bash Idioms
Write Powerful, Flexible, Readable Shell Scripts

Carl Albing and JP Vossen

Beijing · Boston · Farnham · Sebastopol · Tokyo

bash Idioms

by Carl Albing and JP Vossen

Published by O'Reilly Media, Inc., 1005 Gravenstein Highway North, Sebastopol, CA 95472.

O'Reilly books may be purchased for educational, business, or sales promotional use. Online editions are also available for most titles (*https://oreilly.com*). For more information, contact our corporate/institutional sales department: 800-998-9938 or *corporate@oreilly.com*.

Acquisitions Editor: Suzanne McQuade
Development Editor: Nicole Taché
Production Editor: Kristen Brown
Copyeditor: Piper Editorial Consulting, LLC

Proofreader: Liz Wheeler
Indexer: nSight, Inc.
Interior Designer: David Futato
Cover Designer: Karen Montgomery

March 2022:   First Edition

Revision History for the First Edition

2022-03-16:   First Release

See *https://oreilly.com/catalog/errata.csp?isbn=9781492094753* for release details.

978-1-492-09475-3

[LSI]

Table of Contents

Preface

Webster's Dictionary defines *idiom* as:[1]

> 1: an expression in the usage of a language that is peculiar to itself either in having a meaning that cannot be derived from the conjoined meanings of its elements (such as up in the air for "undecided") or in its grammatically atypical use of words (such as give way)
>
> 2a: the language peculiar to a people or to a district, community, or class: dialect
>
> 2b: the syntactical, grammatical, or structural form peculiar to a language
>
> 3: a style or form of artistic expression that is characteristic of an individual, a period or movement, or a medium or instrument

Why *bash Idioms*? One word—readability. Or perhaps a different word—understandability. In this book, those words mean the same thing. We don't have to convince you that readability is critically important; unless this is the first book about programming you are reading,[2] you already get it. *Readability* means being able to read and understand code, especially code that someone else wrote, but it also means being able to write code that you, or someone else, can later read and understand. Clearly these aspects are different sides of the same coin, so we'll explore both the clear idioms to use and the obscure ones to avoid.

We think of bash, informally, as a language to use to "run things." If you need to do a lot of heavy data processing, bash may not be the first choice. You can do it, but it might not be pretty. Of course, if you already have the data processing tools you need and you just have to "glue" them together, well, then bash is great. But if all we do is run things, why do we care about the idioms of the language or its "structural form"? Programs grow, features creep, things change, and there is nothing more permanent

---

1 See *https://oreil.ly/pgx8b*, as viewed on 2022-03-07.

2 If you are new to programming or bash, you may want to start with *Learning the bash Shell* or the *bash Cookbook* (both O'Reilly) and come back to this book later.

than a "temporary solution." Sooner or later someone is going to have to read the code, understand it, and make changes. If it's written using an obscure idiom, the job is that much harder.

In a lot of ways, bash doesn't look like other languages. It has a lot of history (some may say "baggage"), and there are reasons it looks and works the way it does. We're not going to talk about that very much, because we cover a lot of that in the *bash Cookbook*. Shell scripts arguably "run the world," at least in the Unix and Linux worlds (and Linux pretty much runs the cloud world), and a huge majority of those scripts are interpreted by bash. Maintaining backward compatibility back to the very first Unix shells is critically important, but it imposes some…restrictions.

Then there are the dialects. The big one, especially for backward compatibility, is POSIX (*https://oreil.ly/jWTKj*). We won't talk too much about that either—after all, this is *bash Idioms*, not *POSIX Idioms*. Other dialects may appear when programmers write bash code in a style that is more characteristic of another language they know. A flow that makes sense in C may feel clumsy or disjointed in bash, though. So with this book, we intend to demonstrate a "style or form of…expression that is characteristic" of bash (in the spirit of the third definition in Webster's Dictionary). Python programmers talk about their style as "pythonic." We'd like this book to illustrate and illuminate code that is "bashy."

By the end of this book the reader will be able to do the following:

- Write useful, flexible, and readable bash code…with style
- Decode bash idioms such as ${MAKEMELC,,} and ${PATHNAME##*/}
- Save time and ensure consistency when automating tasks
- Amaze and impress colleagues with bash idioms
- Discover how bash idioms can make your code clean and concise

Running bash

We're going to assume you are already programming in bash, and therefore you don't need to learn where to find or install it. Of course, bash is *just there* in almost all Linux distributions, and already there by default or installable on virtually any other operating system. You can get it in Windows using "Git for Windows" (*https://gitforwindows.org*), Windows Subsystem for Linux (WSL) (*https://oreil.ly/8ijiP*), or various other options we cover in the *bash Cookbook*.

bash on Mac

That said, watch out for stock bash on a Mac; it's quite old, and many newer idioms (v4+) won't work. You can obtain a newer version by installing MacPorts, Homebrew, or Fink and looking for bash. According to Apple (*https://oreil.ly/2PZRm*), the issue is that newer versions of bash use GPLv3, which is a problem for Apple.

On a related note, Apple also says (*https://oreil.ly/PyKl4*) that macOS Catalina and newer will use Zsh as the default login and interactive shell. Zsh is mostly compatible with bash, but some code in this book won't work unmodified. On Macs, bash isn't going away (yet, at least), and having Zsh as your default shell will not affect a bash "shebang" line (see "Shebang!" on page 94), but again, unless *you* upgrade, you'll be stuck with stone-age bash.

We've tagged example scripts "Does not work on Zsh 5.4.2" as a best-effort clue for Mac users, but this is a book about bash, so we're going to stay focused.

bash in Containers

Be careful in Docker or other containers where /bin/sh is not bash and /bin/bash may not even exist! This applies to Internet of Things and other constrained environments such as industrial controllers.

/bin/sh may be bash in "POSIX" mode, but it may also be Ash or Dash (*https://oreil.ly/CUwhu*), or BusyBox (which is probably actually Dash), or maybe even something else. You'll need to be specific (see also "Shebang!" on page 94) and possibly either ensure that bash is actually installed or stick to POSIX and avoid "bashisms."

Revision Control

We sincerely hope you are already using some kind of revision control system, so if you are, you can skip this paragraph. If you are not, you should start immediately. We cover all of that in an entire appendix in the *bash Cookbook* (*https://github.com/vossenjp/bashidioms-examples/blob/main/bcb2-appd.pdf*), but there are huge amounts of information about that on the internet, including one author's thoughts on the subject (*https://oreil.ly/fPHy8*). Go figure something out; we'll wait.

Hello World

In many other resources, you have to wait until the end of chapter 1 or maybe even chapter 2 or 3 before you get to "Hello World," but we're going to jump right in! Since you are already writing bash code and keeping it in revision control (right?), talking about echo 'Hello, World' would be pretty silly, so we won't. Oops.

Conventions Used in This Book

The following typographical conventions are used in this book:

Italic
> Indicates new terms, URLs, email addresses, filenames, and file extensions.

`Constant width`
> Used for program listings, as well as within paragraphs to refer to program elements such as variable or function names, databases, data types, environment variables, statements, and keywords.

`Constant width bold`
> Shows commands or other text that should be typed literally by the user.

`Constant width italic`
> Shows text that should be replaced with user-supplied values or by values determined by context.

 This element signifies a tip or suggestion.

 This element signifies a general note.

 This element indicates a warning or caution.

Using Code Examples

Supplemental material (code examples, exercises, etc.) is available for download at *https://github.com/vossenjp/bashidioms-examples*.

If you have a technical question or a problem using the code examples, please send email to *bookquestions@oreilly.com*.

This book is here to help you get your job done. In general, if example code is offered with this book, you may use it in your programs and documentation. You do not need to contact us for permission unless you're reproducing a significant portion of the code. For example, writing a program that uses several chunks of code from this book does not require permission. Selling or distributing examples from O'Reilly books does require permission. Answering a question by citing this book and quoting example code does not require permission. Incorporating a significant amount of example code from this book into your product's documentation does require permission.

We appreciate, but generally do not require, attribution. An attribution usually includes the title, author, publisher, and ISBN. For example: "*bash Idioms* by Carl Albing and JP Vossen (O'Reilly). Copyright 2022 Carl Albing and JP Vossen, 978-1-492-09475-3."

If you feel your use of code examples falls outside fair use or the permission given above, feel free to contact us at *permissions@oreilly.com*.

O'Reilly Online Learning

O'REILLY®   For more than 40 years, *O'Reilly Media* has provided technology and business training, knowledge, and insight to help companies succeed.

Our unique network of experts and innovators share their knowledge and expertise through books, articles, conferences, and our online learning platform. O'Reilly's online learning platform gives you on-demand access to live training courses, in-depth learning paths, interactive coding environments, and a vast collection of text and video from O'Reilly and 200+ other publishers. For more information, please visit *https://oreilly.com*.

How to Contact Us

Please address comments and questions concerning this book to the publisher:

O'Reilly Media, Inc.
1005 Gravenstein Highway North
Sebastopol, CA 95472
800-998-9938 (in the United States or Canada)
707-829-0515 (international or local)
707-829-0104 (fax)

We have a web page for this book, where we list errata, examples, and any additional information. You can access this page at *https://oreil.ly/bashIdioms*.

Email *bookquestions@oreilly.com* to comment or ask technical questions about this book.

For more information about our books, courses, conferences, and news, see our website at *https://www.oreilly.com*.

Find us on Facebook: *https://facebook.com/oreilly*.

Follow us on Twitter: *https://twitter.com/oreillymedia*.

Watch us on YouTube: *https://www.youtube.com/oreillymedia*.

Acknowledgments

bash

Thank you to the GNU Software Foundation and Brian Fox for writing bash. And a very big thank-you to Chet Ramey, who has been maintaining and improving bash since around version 1.14 in the early to mid-1990s. You (plural) have given us a great tool that has helped in so many ways.

Reviewers

Many thanks to our reviewers, Doug McIlroy, Ian Miell, Curtis Old, and Paul Troncone! They all provided valuable feedback, suggestions, and in some cases alternate solutions, pointed out issues we had overlooked, and in general greatly improved the book. Any errors or omissions in this text are ours and not theirs.

O'Reilly

Thanks to the entire team at O'Reilly, without whom this book would not exist (for many reasons)—and if it did, the content wouldn't be or look nearly as good!

Thanks to Mike Loukides for the original idea and for asking us and trusting us to run with it. Thanks to Suzanne "Zan" McQuade for helping to flesh it out. Many thanks to Nicole Taché for editing, sanity checks, and generally putting up with us during the long writing process and to Kristen Brown for all the same things during the production process. Special thanks to Nick Adams in Tools for fixing our many (egregious) AsciiDoc bugs, and other above and beyond tool-chain help. Thank you also to Kim Sandoval (copyeditor), Cheryl Lenser (indexer), Liz Wheeler (proofreader), David Futato (interior design), Karen Montgomery (cover design), and the rest of the great team at O'Reilly.

From Carl

Thanks to JP for all his work on this, his thoroughness, his attention to detail, and his willingness to put up with me. Thanks to all the O'Reilly people for helping to bring this to realization.

My work on this book is dedicated to my wife, Cynthia, who puts up with my strange hours when I'm writing and pretends, convincingly, to be interested in what I'm writing about. My work on this book is meant, as we say at Bethel University, for God's glory and my neighbor's good.

From JP

Thanks to Carl for all his work; we seem to have managed complementary schedules again. Thanks to Mike for getting the ball rolling (again) and to Nicole for keeping it rolling and her patience with our work, life, and time management issues.

This book is dedicated to my wife, Karen, who is the executive vice president in charge of all the things, without whom my life would not function. Thanks for your incredible support, patience, and understanding. Finally, thanks to Kate and Sam, for taking "unless you're bleeding or on fire, I've got book stuff to do" for an answer.

## CHAPTER 1

A Big "if" Idiom

To get you started in understanding bash idioms, we'll look at a bash construct that allows you to do what you might normally do with an if/then/else construct but with sparser syntax. The idiomatic expression we'll show you in this chapter has some real advantages—mostly terseness—and some pitfalls to avoid. But if you don't know bash idioms, you might not recognize or realize what is going on.

Take a look at this piece of code:

```
[[ -n "$DIR" ]] && cd "$DIR"
```

Do you think that looks like an if statement? If you're conversant in bash, you'll recognize that it is functionally the same thing; you'll understand it as an if statement even though the if keyword doesn't appear in the code.

What's going on?

The Big "if"

To explain this idiom, let's first look at a similar but simpler example:

```
cd tmp && rm scratchfile
```

This too, is, in effect, an if statement. If the cd command succeeds, then (and only then) execute the rm command. The "idiom" here is the use of the double ampersand (&&), typically read as "and," to separate the two commands.

Logic or philosophy classes teach the rule: the expression "A AND B" is true if and only if both A and B are each true. Therefore if A is false, there is no need to even consider the value of B. For example, consider "I own a dog AND I own a cat." If I do not own a dog, then this compound expression is false for me, regardless of my cat situation.

Let's apply this to bash. Remember that the basic function of bash is to execute programs. The first part of this statement has the cd command execute. Similar to the logic of the AND, if this first command fails, bash will not bother to execute the second part, the rm command.

The use of the && is meant to remind you of the AND behavior. Bash isn't actually performing an "AND" operation on these two results. (If this were C/C++, that would be a different story, though the conditional execution is the same.) However, this bash idiom does provide the conditional execution of the second command—it isn't run if the first command fails.

Let's go back and look at the original example we gave, namely this expression:

```
[[ -n "$DIR" ]] && cd "$DIR"
```

Do you think you "get it" now? The first expression tests to see if the length of the value of the variable called DIR is nonzero. If it has a value, that is, if its length is nonzero—and only if it's nonzero—the cd command will attempt to change into a directory named by the value of DIR.

We could have written this as an explicit if statement:

```
if [[ -n "$DIR" ]]; then
    cd "$DIR"
fi
```

To someone less familiar with bash, this latter format is certainly more readable and easily understood. But there isn't much going on inside the then clause, just the cd command, so it seems a bit "bulky" in its syntax. You'll have to decide which to use based on who your readers will likely be and how likely other commands would be added inside the then clause. We'll offer more opinions on this topic in the sections that follow.

 bash Help

The bash help command is great for any builtin command (*https://oreil.ly/NQAaZ*), but help test provides especially helpful clues about the test expression, like -n. You might also check man bash, but if you do, you'll want to search for "conditional expressions." The bash man page is very long; help *thing* has much shorter, focused topics. If you are not sure if the command in question is a bash builtin, just try it with the help command, or use type -a *thing* to find out.

Admittedly, knowing that help test will tell you what -n means is tricky, but then, you were smart enough to buy this book, so now you know. Here is another subtle little tidbit; go try this: help [. You're welcome.

Or ELSE…

A similar idiom is available using the || characters to separate two items in a bash list. Pronounced "or," the second part will execute only if the first part fails. This is meant to remind you of the logic rule for "OR," as in: A OR B. The whole expression is true if either A is true or B is true. Put another way, if A is true, it doesn't matter if B is true or false. For example, consider the phrase "I own a dog OR I own a cat." If I do, in fact, own a dog, then this expression is true for me regardless of my cat situation.

Applying this to bash:

```
[[ -z "$DIR" ]] || cd "$DIR"
```

Do you think you can explain this one? If the variable is of length zero, then the first part is "true," so there is no need to execute the second half; no cd command will be run. But if the length of $DIR is nonzero, the test would return "false," so only then would we run the cd command.

You might read the line of bash as "Either $DIR is zero length, OR we attempt to cd into that directory."

To write that as an explicit if statement is a bit odd, as there is no then action to be taken. The code after the || is like the else clause:

```
if [[ -z "$DIR" ]]; then
    :
else
    cd "$DIR"
fi
```

The ":" is a null statement in shell—so it does nothing in that case.

In summary: two commands separated by an && are like an if and its then clause; two commands separated by a || are like an if and its else clause.

More than One

You might want to do more than one thing in this else-like clause after the || (or in a then-like clause after an &&) and therein lies a danger. It might be tempting to write something like this:

```
# Caution: not what you might think!
cd /tmp || echo "cd to /tmp failed." ;  exit
```

The "or" connection tells us that if the cd fails we will execute the echo command, telling the user that the cd failed. But here's the catch: the exit will happen regardless. Not what you expected, right?

Think of the semicolon as equivalent to a newline, and it all becomes much clearer (and more obviously not what you wanted):

```
cd /tmp || echo "cd to /tmp failed."
exit
```

How can we get the behavior we want? We can group the echo and exit together so that they are, taken together, the clause on the righthand side of the "or," like this:

```
# Succeed with the cd or bail with a message
cd /tmp || { echo "cd to /tmp failed." ;  exit ; }
```

The braces are bash syntax for a compound command, i.e., grouping statements together. You may have seen something similar using parentheses, but using parentheses executes the statements in a subshell (*https://oreil.ly/lZnvi*), also referred to as a child process. That would incur an overhead we don't need, and the exit occurring from within a subshell wouldn't accomplish much either.

Closing Compound Commands

A quirk of bash requires a specific syntax for how you close the compound command. It must end with either a semicolon or a newline before the closing brace. If you use a semicolon, there needs to be whitespace before the brace so that the brace can be recognized as a reserved word (otherwise it gets confused with the closing brace of shell variable syntax, as in ${VAR}, for example). That is why the preceding example ends with what looks to be an extraneous semicolon: { echo "..." ; exit ; }. Using a newline, that final semicolon isn't needed:

```
# Succeed with the cd or bail with a message
cd /tmp || { echo "cd to /tmp failed." ;  exit
           }
```

but that might not read as cleanly. At the left edge, it seems oddly placed; indented with whitespace, it groups more logically but seems bare.

We recommend you stick with the extra semicolon, and don't forget the space between it and the closing brace.

More than One Again

What if you need more complex logic? What about multiple AND and OR constructs? How are they handled? What do you think the following line of code will do?

```
[ -n "$DIR" ] && [ -d "$DIR" ] && cd "$DIR" || exit 4
```

If the DIR variable is not empty and the file named by the DIR variable is a directory, then it will cd to that directory; otherwise it will exit from the script, returning a 4.

That does what you might have expected—but maybe not for the reason you think. You might, from this example, be tempted to think that the && has higher precedence than the || operator, but it doesn't. They're just grouping from left to right. The syntax for bash says that the && and || operators are of equal precedence and are left associative. Need convincing? Look at these examples:

```
$ echo 1 && echo 2 || echo 3
1
2
$
```

but also:

```
$ echo 1 || echo 2 && echo 3
1
3
$
```

Notice that it always evaluates the leftmost operator regardless of whether it's AND or OR; it's not operator precedence but simple left associativity that determines the order of evaluation.

Don't Do This

While we're on the subject of if statements (or how not to use them), here's an example of an explicit if that you may see quite often in older scripts. We show it to you here so that we can explain the idiom but also to urge you never to imitate this style. Here's the code:

```
### Don't write your if statements to check like this
if [ $VAR"X" = X ]; then
    echo empty
fi

### Or this
if [ "x$VAR" == x ]; then
    echo empty
fi

### Or other variations on this theme
```

Don't do this. What are they doing in this code? They're checking to see if the variable VAR is empty. They do that by appending the value of VAR with some character (here X). If the resulting string matches just the letter itself, then the variable was empty. Don't do this.

There are better ways to make this check. Here's a simple alternative:

```
# Is the length of the variable zero? i.e., empty or null
if [[ -z "$VAR" ]]; then
    echo empty
fi
```

Single Versus Double Brackets

This example of what not to do uses the single brackets, [and], to surround the condition that they are testing. That's *not* what we're asking you to avoid. We want you to avoid the string append and comparison; instead, use the -z or -n to make these tests. So why have our examples all used double brackets, [[and]], for our if (and non-if) statements? They are an addition to bash (not in the original sh command), and they avoid some confusing edge case behaviors that single brackets exhibit (variable inside quotes or not). We showed this example with single brackets as this type of comparison is often seen in older scripts. You may need to stay with single brackets, if your goal is portability across various platforms and/or to non-bash platforms (e.g., dash). As a side note, the double brackets are keywords, whereas the left single bracket is a builtin, a difference that may explain some subtle differences in behaviors. Our advice remains to use the double-bracket syntax except when unavoidable.

You can check for the opposite case, checking to see if the length of the string is nonzero, by using the -n option or by just referencing the variable:

```
# This checks for a nonzero length, i.e., not empty, not null
if [[ -n "$VAR" ]]; then
    echo "VAR has a value:" $VAR
fi
```

```
# Same here
if [[ "$VAR" ]]; then
    echo even easier this way
fi
```

So you see there is no need to use that other approach, which was necessary in legacy versions of the test command ("[") that are rarely used anymore. We thought you ought to see it, though, so you'll recognize it in older scripts. Now you also know a better way to write it.

Style and Readability: Recap

In this chapter we took a look at a particular bash idiom—the "no-if" `if` statement. It doesn't look like a traditional `if/then/else`, but it can behave exactly like one. Unless this is something you recognize, some scripts that you read might remain obscure. This idiom is also worth using to check that any necessary preconditions are in place before executing a command, or to make a short error check without disrupting the flow of the main logic of the script.

By using `&&` and `||` operators, you can write `if/then/else` logic without the use of those familiar keywords. But bash does have `if`, `then`, and `else` as keywords. So when do you use them, and when do you use the shorthand? The answer comes down to readability.

For complex logic, it makes the most sense to use the familiar keywords. But, for simple test and check situations with single actions, using the `&&` and `||` operators can be very convenient and will not distract from the main flow of logic. Use `help test` to remind you which tests you can use, like `-n -r`, and consider copying the help text into a comment for the future.

In either case, for familiar `if` statements or idiomatic "no-if" statements, we encourage the use of the double-bracket syntax.

Now that you've seen one bash idiom in depth, let's take a look at others and really up your bash game.

## CHAPTER 2

Looping Lingo

It's not just C-style for loops—bash includes other syntaxes and styles; some are more familiar to Python programmers, but each has its place. There is a for loop with no apparent arguments, useful in both scripts and inside functions. There's also an iterator-like for loop with explicit values and values that can come from other commands.

Looping Constructs

Looping constructs are common in programming languages. Since the invention of the C language, many programming languages have adopted the C-style for loop. It's such a powerful, readable construct because it groups the initialization code, the termination condition, and the iteration code all into one place. For example, in C (or Java, or...):

```
/* NOT bash */
for (i=0; i<10; i++) {
    printf("%d\n", i);
}
```

With just a few minor syntax differences, bash follows much the same approach:

```
for ((i=0; i<10; i++)); do
    printf '%d\n' "$i"
done
```

Note, especially, the use of double parentheses. Rather than braces, bash uses do and done to enclose the statements of the loop. As with C/C++, an idiomatic use of the for loop is the empty for loop, giving a deliberate infinite loop (you'll also see while true; do):

```
for ((;;)); do
    printf 'forever'
done
```

But that's not the only kind of for loop in bash. Here's a common idiom in shell scripts:

```
for value; do
    echo "$value"
    # Do more stuff with $value...
done
```

This looks like something is missing, doesn't it? Where does value get its values? This won't do anything for you on the command line, but if you use this in a shell script, then the for loop will iterate over the parameters to the script. That is, it will use $1, then $2, then $3, and so on, as the values for value.

Put that for loop in a file called myloop.sh, then you can run it like this and see the three arguments ("-c", "17", and "core") printed out:

```
$ bash myloop.sh -c 17 core
-c
17
core
$
```

This abbreviated for loop is also very often found in function definitions:

```
function Listem {
    for arg; do
        echo "arg to func: '$arg'"
    done
    echo "Inside func: \$0 is still: '$0'"
}
```

Inside a function definition, the parameters $1, $2, etc., are the parameters to the function and not parameters to the enclosing shell script. Therefore, inside the function definition, the for loop will iterate over the parameters passed to the function.

This minimalist for loop iterates over an implied list of values—the parameters passed either to the script or the function. When used in the main body of a script, it iterates over the parameters that were passed to the script; when used inside a shell function, it iterates over the parameters that were passed to that function.

This is definitely one of the obscure bash idioms. You need to know how to read it, but we'll circle back to debate how to write it in a later section (spoiler alert: like Python says, explicit is better than implicit).

We might like a similarly simple loop but one with explicit values of our own choosing not limited to the parameters—bash has just the thing.

Explicit Values

In bash, the `for` loop can be given a list of values to loop over, like this:

```
for num in 1 2 3 4 5; do
    echo "$num"
done
```

Since bash is dealing with strings, we aren't restricted to numbers:

```
for person in Sue Neil Pat Harry; do
    echo $person
done
```

Of course, the list of values can include variables as well as literals:

```
for person in $ME $3 Pat ${RA[2]} Sue; do
    echo $person
done
```

Another source of values for the `for` loop can come from other commands, either a single command or a pipeline of commands:

```
for arg in $(some cmd or other | sort -u)
```

Examples of this kind are:

```
for arg in $(cat /some/file)
for arg in $(< /some/file)     # Faster than shelling out to cat
for pic in $(find . -name '*.jpg')
for val in $(find . -type d | LC_ALL=C sort)
```

A common use, especially in older scripts, is something like this:

```
for i in $(seq 1 10)
```

because the `seq` command will generate a sequence of numbers. This case could be considered equivalent to:

```
for ((i = 1; i <= 10; i++))
```

This latter `for` is more efficient and probably more readable. (Note that after the loop terminates, however, the value of i will differ between those two forms [10 versus 11], though generally one doesn't use the value outside of the loop.)

There's also this variation, but it has bash version portability issues because the brace expansion was introduced in v3.0 and zero-padding of expanded numeric values was introduced in v4.0:

```
for i in {01..10}; do echo "$i"; done
```

Leading Zeros

When either of the first two terms starts with a zero in a {start..end..inc} brace expansion, it will force each output value to be the same width—using zeros to pad them on the left side in bash v4.0 or newer. So {098..100} will result in: 098 099 100, whereas {98..0100} will pad to four characters, resulting in: 0098 0099 0100.

This brace expansion construct can be especially useful when you want the numbers that are being generated to be part of a larger string. You simply put the brace construct as part of the string. For example, if you want to generate five filenames like log01.txt through log05.txt, you could write:

```
for filename in log{01..5}.txt ; do
    # Do something with the filenames here
    echo $filename
done
```

Braces Versus printf -v

You could also do this with a numeric for loop and then a printf -v to construct the filename from the numbers, but the brace expansion seems a bit simpler. Use the numeric for loop and printf when you need the numeric values for something else in addition to the filenames.

The seq command, though, can still be very useful for generating a sequence of floating-point style numbers. You specify an increment between the starting and ending values:

```
for value in $(seq 2.1 0.3 3.2); do
    echo $value
done
```

would yield:

```
2.1
2.4
2.7
3.0
```

Just remember that bash doesn't do floating point arithmetic. You may want to generate these values to pass to some other program from within your script.

Similar to Python

Here's another common phrase seen in `for` loops in bash:

```
for person in ${name_list[@]}; do
    echo $person
done
```

which might produce output like this:

```
Arthur
Ann
Henry
John
```

Looking at that example, you might be tempted to think that this bash `for` loop is like Python, where it can iterate over values returned by an iterator object. Well, bash is iterating over a series of values in this example, but those values don't come from an iterator object. Instead the names are all spelled out before the looping begins.

The construct `${name_list[@]}` is bash syntax for listing all the values of a bash array, henceforth called a *list*. (See the terminology discussion in the introduction to Chapter 7. In this example, the list is called `name_list`.) A substitution is made by bash as it prepares the command to be run. So the `for` loop doesn't see the list syntax; the substitution happens first. What the `for` loop gets looks just as if we typed the values explicitly:

```
for person in Arthur Ann Henry John
```

What about dictionaries? What Python calls "dictionaries," bash refers to as "associative arrays" and what others call "key/value pairs" or "hashes" (again, see the introduction to Chapter 7). The construct `${hash[@]}` works fine for the values of the key/value pairs. To loop over the keys (i.e., indices) of the hash, add an exclamation point. The construct `${!hash[@]}` can be used, as shown in this code snippet:

```
# We want a hash (i.e., key/value pairs)
declare -A hash
# Read in our data
while read key value; do
    hash[$key]="$value"
done
# Show us what we've got, though they won't
# likely be in the same order as read
for key in "${!hash[@]}"; do
    echo "key $key ==> value ${hash[$key]}"
done
```

Here's an alternate example:

```
# We want a hash (i.e., key/value pairs)
declare -A hash
# Read in our data: word and # of occurrences
while read word count; do
    let hash[$word]+="$count"
done
# Show us what we've got, though the order
# is based on the hash, i.e., we don't control it
for key in "${!hash[@]}";do
    echo "word $key count = ${hash[$key]}"
done
```

This chapter is more about looping constructs like for, but if you want more details and examples about lists and hashes, see Chapter 7.

Quotes and Spaces

There is one more important aspect to consider about this for loop. Did you catch our inconsistent use of quotes in the preceding example? If the values in the list have spaces in them (for example, if each entry had a first and last name), then our example for loop:

```
for person in ${namelist[@]}; do
    echo $person
done
```

might produce output like this:

```
Art
Smith
Ann
Arundel
Hank
Till
John
Jakes
```

The for loop prints out eight different values for the four names in our list. Why? How? The answer lies in the substitution that bash makes for ${namelist[@]}. It just puts those names in place of the variable expression. That leaves eight words in the list, like this:

```
for person in Art Smith Ann Arundel Hank Till John Jakes
```

The for loop is just given a list of words. It doesn't know where they came from.

There is bash syntax to solve this dilemma: put quotes around the list expression and each value will be quoted.

```
for person in "${namelist[@]}"
```

will be translated to:

```
for person in "Art Smith" "Ann Arundel" "Hank Till" "John Jakes"
```

and that will yield the desired result:

```
Art Smith
Ann Arundel
Hank Till
John Jakes
```

If your for loop is going to iterate over a list of filenames, then you should be sure to use the quotation marks, since filenames might have a space in them.

There is one last twist to all this. The list syntax can use either * or @ to list all the elements of the list: ${namelist[*]} works just as well...*except* when put inside quotes. The expression:

```
"${namelist[*]}"
```

will be evaluated with all of the values inside of a single string. In this example:

```
for person in "${namelist[*]}"; do
    echo $person
done
```

would result in a single line of output, like this:

```
Art Smith Ann Arundel Hank Till John Jakes
```

Though a single string might be useful in some contexts, it is especially pointless in a for loop—there would be only one iteration. We recommend using @ unless you are positive that you need *.

See also "Quoting" on page 129.

Developing and Testing for Loops

It turns out that "for list do something" loops are extremely useful in all kinds of ways. Let's take two simple examples: running SSH commands on a list of servers and renaming files, like for file in *.JPEG; do mv -v $file ${file/JPEG/jpg}; done. But how do you develop and test a script or even a simple for command? The same way you develop anything else: start simple and go one step at a time. But in particular, you use echo (see Example 2-1). Note that the bash builtin echo has a number of interesting options, but is not POSIX (see "POSIX Output" on page 56). The most interesting and often used are -e (to enable interpretation of backslash escapes) and -n (to suppress the automatic trailing newline).

Example 2-1. File rename—test version

```
### Building and testing a rename command, note the echo
for file in *.JPEG; do echo mv -v $file ${file/JPEG/jpg}; done

### Simple multi-node SSH, note the 1st echo (can do on 1 line, broken for book)
for node in web-server{00..09}; do
   echo ssh $node 'echo -e "$HOSTNAME\t$(date "+%F") $(uptime)"';
done
```

Once it's working as expected, remove that leading echo and go. Of course, if you are using redirection in the block, you have to be careful about that, perhaps changing | to .p., > to .gt., and so on until you get each stage working.

Execute the Same Command Across Multiple Hosts

This is way out of scope for this book, but if you need to run the same command on many hosts, you should probably be using Ansible, Chef, Puppet, or a similar tool. Sometimes you have a really quick and dirty need, and one of these tools might be useful:

clusterssh
 Written in Perl, it opens a bunch of unmanaged terminals in windows.

mssh (MultiSSH)
 GTK+–based multi-SSH client in a single GUI window.

mussh
 MUltihost SSH Wrapper shell script.

pconsole
 Intended for tiling window managers, spawns a terminal per host.

multixterm
 Written in Expect & Tk, drives multiple xterms.

PAC Manager
 A Perl SecureCRT-like GUI on Linux.

while and until

We mentioned while in passing previously, and it works as you'd expect—"execute block while criteria exit status is zero":

```
while <CRITERIA>; do <BLOCK>; done
```

It's often used in reading files; see several examples in Chapter 9. For argument parsing, see "Parsing Options" on page 75.

Unlike other languages, in bash until is just ! while, or "execute block while criteria exit status is not zero":

```
until <CRITERIA>; do <BLOCK>; done
### Same:
! while <CRITERIA>; do <BLOCK>; done
```

This is really handy for something like waiting for a node to be created or rebooted (Example 2-2).

Example 2-2. Wait for reboot

```
until ssh user@10.10.10.10; do sleep 3; done
```

Style and Readability: Recap

In this chapter, we first took a quick look at the C/C++ style numerical for loop. Then we went further. Bash is very string oriented and has some other styles of for loops worth knowing. Its minimalist loop for variable provides implicit (and arguably obscure) iteration over the arguments to a script or a function. An explicit list of values, string or otherwise, provided to the for loop also gives us the perfect mechanism for iterating over all the elements of a list or over all keys in a hash.

We now know that both ${namelist[@]} and ${namelist[*]} show all the values of the list, but if they are enclosed in double quotes, the result is different: separate strings versus one large string. The same is true for the special shell variables $@ and $*. They both represent the list of all the arguments to the script (i.e., $1, $2, etc.). When enclosed in double quotes, though, they also result in either multiple strings or a single string. Why bring that up now? Only to circle back to our simplest for loop:

```
for param
```

and say that this is equivalent to:

```
for param in "$@"
```

We argue that the second form is better because it shows more explicitly which values are being iterated over. However, there is a counterargument that the $@ variable name itself and the necessity of the quotes are both specialized knowledge that is no more obvious to the naive reader than just the first, simple form. If you really prefer the first form, simply add a comment:

```
for param      # Iterate over all the script arguments
```

When looping over a sequence of integer values, the C-style `for` loop with double parentheses is probably the most readable as well as the most efficient. (If efficiency is a big concern, be sure to use `declare -i i` early in your script to make your variable "i" an explicit integer, avoiding conversion to/from a string.)

Knowing that you have all these values readily available, what might you do with them? What goes on inside the loop, making use of these values? Decisions must be made about the values encountered, and decision-making brings us to another important feature in bash: its supercharged and superflexible `case` statement, the topic of the next chapter.

`for` commands are extremely useful but can be tricky to develop. Start simple and use echo until you're sure your command is working as intended. And remember the "syntactic sugar" `while` and `until` commands for readability where useful.

## CHAPTER 3

Just in CASE

Many programming languages provide a "switch" or "match" statement, an n-way branch, used as an alternative to a string of if/then/else clauses. There is a similar construct in bash: the case statement. It comes with powerful pattern matching and is very useful in scripting.

Make Your Case

The keywords case and in delineate the value you want to compare against various patterns. Here's a simple example:

```
case "$var" in
    yes ) echo "glad you agreed" ;;
    no  )
        echo "sorry; good bye"
        exit
    ;;
    * ) echo "invalid answer. try again" ;;
esac
```

…which you can probably figure out. It checks to see if the value in $var is "yes" or "no" and executes the corresponding statement(s). It even has a default action. The end of the case statement is marked by esac, which is *case* spelled backward. This example is pretty readable, but it just scratches the surface. You'll also note that you used two different block styles, a "one-liner" for yes and a more typical block (closed by ;;…more on that later) for no. Which you use depends on what you are doing and how the code lines up for readability.

(in case

The syntax for the `case` statement includes an optional "(" to match the ")" in the example. For example, we could have written `("yes")` instead of just `"yes")` and similarly for the other items. We've rarely seen this used, though. After all, who wants to type an extra character?

The real power of the `case` statement, and the most idiomatic appearance, comes from using the shell's pattern matching for the various possible value comparisons:

```
case "$var" in

    [Nn][Oo]* )
        echo "Fine. Leave then."
        exit
    ;;
    [Yy]?? | [Ss]ure | [Oo][Kk]* )
        echo "OK. Glad we agree."
    ;;
    * ) echo 'Try again.'
        continue
    ;;
esac
```

Here is a quick review of bash pattern matching, which you are probably familiar with as command line *wildcards* (or *globs* (*https://oreil.ly/AtYU1*)). There are three special characters to watch for: ? matches a single character, * matches any number of characters (including none), and brackets, [ ], match any of the characters included between the brackets.

In our example, the construct [Yy] matches either uppercase *Y* or lowercase *y*. The construct [Nn][Oo]* matches either upper- or lowercase *N*, followed by either upper- or lowercase *O*, followed by any number of any other characters. The pattern matches the following words (and others, too): *no, No, nO, NO, noway, Not Ever*, and *nope*. It will not be a match if the value of $var is the word *never*.

Can you guess some possible values for the affirmative case? The vertical bar separates different patterns that would all lead to the same result. (Think "OR" but not the || or.) The words *Yes, yes, YES, yEs, yES, yup, Sure, sure, OK, ok*, and *OKfine* and "OK why not" would all work. But these words would not: *ya, SURE, oook*, and many more.

The default case isn't special syntax—it's just a pattern—but this pattern would match anything. If no other previous pattern has produced a match, then we know that this one will—it matches any number of any characters. Therefore, bash script writers put this one *last* in the list if they want to catch a default case.

Not RegEx

The pattern matching used in the `case` statement is *not* regular expressions. There is only one place in bash where regular expressions (regex or regexp) are allowed, and that's in the `if` statement using the `=~` comparison operator. If you really need to use regex, then you need to use a series of `if/then/else` statements instead of `case`.

A Realistic Use Case

Code that parses command line options is a common place to find a `case` statement. Let's look at a simple but somewhat realistic script that makes good use of a `case` statement.

Motivation

If you've ever used Linux or Unix, you've likely made extensive use of the `ls` command to list out filenames and related information. Some options to `ls` are quite handy at giving more information or sorting it in certain ways. You might develop certain habits of how you use `ls` or the options you use most frequently. As a result, you might create some aliases or even entire scripts to make it easier to use your favorite combinations. But then you end up with several distinct scripts. They're all related in functionality but all distinct. How might we combine them all into one script?

Consider a familiar example, the popular source control software called Git. It has several related but distinct functions, all invoked with the one command name `git` but each distinguished by a separate second keyword, for example, `git clone`, `git add`, `git commit`, `git push`, and so forth.

Our Script

We can apply this "subcommand" approach to our situation. Let's consider a few `ls`-related functions that we'd like to use: listing the files in order of filename length (along with the length), listing just the longest filename, listing the last few most recently modified files, and listing filenames with color coding indicating file type—a standard feature of `ls` but one that requires a few hard-to-remember options.

Our script will be named `list`, but there will be a second word to specify one of these functions. That word could be `color`, `last`, `length`, or `long`. Example 3-1 contains a script that does that.

Example 3-1. Simple wrapper script using case

```bash
#!/usr/bin/env bash
# list.sh: A wrapper script for ls-related tools & simple `case..esac` demo
# Original Author & date: _bash Idioms_ 2022
# bash Idioms filename: examples/ch03/list.sh
#_____
VERSION='v1.2b'

function Usage_Exit {
    echo "$0 [color|last|len|long]"
    exit
}

# Show each filename preceded by the length of its name, sorted by filename
# length.  Note '-' is valid but uncommon in function names, but it is not
# valid in variable names.  We don't usually use it, but you can.
function Ls-Length {
    ls -1 "$@" | while read fn; do
        printf '%3d %s\n' ${#fn} ${fn}
    done | sort -n
}

(( $# < 1 )) && Usage_Exit                                           ❶
sub=$1
shift

case $sub in
    color)                          # Colorized ls
        ls -N --color=tty -T 0 "$@"
    ;;

    last | latest)                  # Latest files               ❷
        ls -lrt | tail "-n${1:-5}"                                ❸
    ;;

    len*)                           # Files with name lengths    ❹
        Ls-Length "$@"
    ;;

    long)                           # File with longest name
        Ls-Length "$@" | tail -1
    ;;

    *)                              # Default
        echo "unknown command: $sub"
        Usage_Exit
    ;;
esac
```

We won't explain all the parts of this script here, though by the end of this book, you will have learned about all the features used. We want to focus mainly on the `case` statement:

❶ Do you recognize the non-if if logic? If not, (re)read Chapter 1.

❷ This is a simple "or" choice between two words.

❸ Use `tail -n5` as the default if a value is not given in `$1`; see "Default Values" on page 38.

❹ This pattern will match any word that begins with "len," so either "len" or "length" with match, but so will "lenny" and "lens." It then calls the `Ls-Length` function (which we defined in the script), passing it all the command line arguments (if any) supplied to this script.

Wrapper Scripts

Everyone has a lot going on, and a lot to remember, so when you can automate or write a script to remember details for you, that's a win. We showed one way to do a "wrapper script" in Example 3-1, but there are a number of interesting variations and tricks that you can use depending on the complexity of the problem you are solving or details you are "remembering." In Example 3-1, we called a function or just put the code inline. That works best with very short code blocks, which in our experience are quite common in these kinds of wrapper scripts. If you have a more complicated solution, or you are working with existing tools, you can call those or a sub-script instead, though you need to tweak the error-checking and possibly usage options. You can also combine that with "Drop-in Directories" on page 93 and source all the "modules" from a directory, perhaps to delegate maintenance of parts of the code to other people or teams.

This larger example is actually a simplified and excerpted version of a script we used while writing this book. AsciiDoc is cool, but we work with a lot of markup languages and they all blur together, so we can write a tool to remember things for us, shown in Example 3-2.

Example 3-2. Complex wrapper script using case

```
#!/usr/bin/env bash
# wrapper.sh: Simple "wrapper" script demo
# Original Author & date: _bash Idioms_ 2022
# bash Idioms filename: examples/ch03/wrapper.sh
#_____

# Trivial Sanity Checks                              ❶
```

```
[ -n "$BOOK_ASC" ] || {
    echo "FATAL: export \$BOOK_ASC to the location of the Asciidoc files!"
    exit 1
}
\cd "$BOOK_ASC" || {
    echo "FATAL: can't cd to '$BOOK_ASC'!"
    exit 2
}

SELF="$0"                                                        ❷

action="$1"                                                      ❸
shift                                                            ❹
[ -x /usr/bin/xsel -a $# -lt 1 ] && {                            ❺
    # Read/write the clipboard on Linux
    text=$(xsel -b)
    function Output {
        echo -en "$*" | xsel -bi
    }
} || {
    # Read/write STDIN/STDOUT
    text=$*
    function Output {
        echo -en "$*"
    }
}

case "$action" in                                                ❻

    ####################################################################
    # Content/Markup                                              ❼

    ### Headers                                                   ❽
    h1 )                    # Inside chapter heading 1 (really AsciiDoc h3) ❾
        Output "[[$($SELF id $text)]]\n=== $text"                ❿
    ;;
    h2 )                    # Inside chapter heading 2 (really AsciiDoc h4)
        Output "[[$($SELF id $text)]]\n==== $text"
    ;;
    h3 )                    # Inside chapter heading 3 (really AsciiDoc h5)
        Output "[[$($SELF id $text)]]\n===== $text"
    ;;

    ### Lists
    bul|bullet )            # Bullet list (** = level 2, + = multiline element)
        Output "* $text"
    ;;
    nul|number|order* )  # Numbered/ordered list (.. = level 2, + = multiline)
        Output ". $text"
    ;;
    term )               # Terms
        Output "term_here::\n $text"
```

```
    ;;

### Inline
bold )                  # Inline bold (O'Reilly prefers italics to bold)
    Output "*$text*"
;;
i|italic*|itl )         # Inline italics (O'Reilly prefers italics to bold)
    Output "_${text}_"
;;
c|constant|cons )       # Inline constant width (command, code, keywords, more)
    Output "+$text+"
;;
type|constantbold )     # Inline bold constant width (user types literally)
    Output "*+$text+*"
;;
var|constantitalic )    # Inline italic constant width (user-supplied values)
    Output "_++$text++_"
;;
sub|subscript )         # Inline subscript
    Output "~$text~"
;;
sup|superscript )       # Inline superscript
    Output "^$text^"
;;
foot )                  # Create a footnote
    Output "footnote:[$text]"
;;
url|link )              # Create a URL with alternate text
    Output "link:\$\$$text\$\$[]"    # URL[link shows as]
;;
esc|escape )            # Escape a character (esp. *)
    Output "\$\$$text\$\$"    # $$*$$
;;


######################################################################
# Tools                                                           ⓫

id )                    ## Convert a hack/recipe name to an ID
    #us_text=${text// /_} # Space to '_'
    #lc_text=${us_text,,} # Lowercase; bash 4+ only!
    # Initial `tr -s '_' ' '` to preserve _ in case we process an ID
    # twice (like from "xref")
    # Also note you can break long lines with a trailing \      ⓬
    Output $(echo $text | tr -s '_' ' ' | tr '[:upper:]' '[:lower:]' \
      | tr -d '[:punct:]' | tr -s ' ' '_')
;;

index )                 ## Creates 'index.txt' in AsciiDoc dir
    # Like:
        # ch02.asciidoc:== The Text Utils
        # ch02.asciidoc:=== Common Text Utils and similar tools
```

```
          # ch02.asciidoc:=== Finding data
        egrep '^=== ' ch*.asciidoc | egrep -v '^ch00.asciidoc' \
          > $BOOK_ASC/index.txt && {
            echo "Updated: $BOOK_ASC/index.txt"
            exit 0
        } || {
            echo "FAILED to update: $BOOK_ASC/index.txt"
            exit 1
        }
    ;;

    rerun )               ## Run examples to re-create (existing!) output files
        # Only re-run for code that ALREADY HAS a *.out file...not ALL *.sh code
        for output in examples/*/*.out; do
            code=${output/out/sh}
            echo "Re-running code for: $code > $output"
            $code > $output
        done
    ;;

    cleanup )             ## Clean up all the xHTML/XML/PDF cruft
        rm -fv {ch??,app?}.{pdf,xml,html} book.{xml,html} docbook-xsl.css
    ;;


    * )
        \cd -  # UGLY cheat to revert the 'cd' above...
        ( echo "Usage:"
        egrep '\)[[:space:]]+# '   $0
        echo ''
        egrep '\)[[:space:]]+## '  $0
        echo ''
        egrep '\)[[:space:]]+### ' $0 ) | grep "${1:-.}" | more
    ;;

esac
```

We've got a lot going on in there, so let's unpack it all:

❶ The real script does a lot of operations on the AsciiDoc source code for this book, so it's just easier to make sure we're in the right place and that we have a handy environment variable set.

❷ We usually use $PROGRAM to hold a bash basename, but in this case we're going to be calling this script recursively a lot, so $SELF just seemed more intuitive.

❸ As we'll discuss more in Chapter 11, using meaningful variable names instead of positional arguments is a good idea, so let's do that.

❹ And once we've captured the action, we don't need the old `$1` anymore, but there might be more options, so `shift $1` away.

❺ If `/usr/bin/xsel` exists and is executable, and if there are no more options, we know we're reading and writing from the X Window clipboard, otherwise we're getting text from the arguments and sending output to STDOUT. In practice, we copy from an editor, switch to the command line, run the tool, switch back, and paste.

❻ This is where we start actually doing something—that is, figuring out what our "action" is.

❼ For code organization and readability, break actions up into sections; see also **⓫**.

❽ Let's start with markup for headers.

❾ This line is both code and documentation. The `$action` is that we want a top-level (for the book code) header, `h1`. We'll see later how that is also documentation.

❿ Do the work. First, call ourselves to get an AsciiDoc "ID" for the text, then output that ID in double square brackets, followed by a newline, then have the text indented with `===` for the header level, then, finally, call the `Output` function. Hopefully the rest of the code is easy to understand.

⓫ For code organization and readability, break actions up into sections; see also **❼**.

⓬ You can break long lines with a trailing `\`; see also "Layout" on page 130.

⓭ Things get interesting again in the catch-all, which combines help or usage with unknown argument handing and a great "search in help" feature.

⓮ We wrap whatever output we have into a subshell we pipe into `more` in case it's long.

⓯ Here's the "line of code as documentation" we talked about in callout **❾**. We `grep` for the closing paren, `)`, from our `case` statement, followed by spaces, followed by a single comment marker, `#`. That gives us our level 1 "Content/Markup" actions. That pulls out the actual lines of code that make the `case` statement work, but it also shows you what it does because of how we've added the comments.

⓰ This does the same for the level 2 "Tools" section.

⑰ This would do the same for level 3, which handles Git operations, but we've omitted that code for simplicity here. But it also uses `grep` with `${1:-.}` to show us help on either something we asked for, like `wrapper.sh help heading`, or everything (`grep "."`). With a script this short, that may not seem like a big deal, but when it grows over time (and it will), that becomes really handy!

The result of the grep commands and the "levels" noted previously is to display a help message that is sorted but grouped into "level 1" and "level 2" sections:

```
$ examples/ch03/wrapper.sh help
Usage:
    h1 )                  # Inside chapter heading 1 (really AsciiDoc h3)
    h2 )                  # Inside chapter heading 2 (really AsciiDoc h4)
    h3 )                  # Inside chapter heading 3 (really AsciiDoc h5)
    bul|bullet )          # Bullet list (** = level 2, + = multiline element)
    nul|number|order* )   # Numbered/ordered list (.. = level 2, + = multiline)
    term )                # Terms
    bold )                # Inline bold (ORA prefers italics to bold)
    i|italic*|itl )       # Inline italics (ORA prefers italics to bold)
    c|constant|cons )     # Inline constant width (command, code, keywords, more)
    type|constantbold )   # Inline bold constant width (user types literally)
    var|constantitalic )  # Inline italic constant width (user-supplied values)
    sub|subscript )       # Inline subscript
    sup|superscript )     # Inline superscript
    foot )                # Create a footnote
    url|link )            # Create a URL with alternate text
    esc|escape )          # Escape a character (esp. *)
    id )                  ## Convert a hack/recipe name to an ID
    index )               ## Creates 'index.txt' in AsciiDoc dir
    rerun )               ## Run examples to re-create (existing!) output files
    cleanup )             ## Clean up all the xHTML/XML/PDF cruft

$ examples/ch03/wrapper.sh help heading
    h1 )                  # Inside chapter heading 1 (really AsciiDoc h3)
    h2 )                  # Inside chapter heading 2 (really AsciiDoc h4)
    h3 )                  # Inside chapter heading 3 (really AsciiDoc h5)
```

One More Twist

At the end of each bit of code associated with a pattern, we ended with a double semicolon. In our first example at the start of this chapter, we wrote:

```
"yes") echo "glad you agreed" ;;
```

After the echo command, we put a `;;`, which indicates that no further action should be taken. Execution will continue after the `esac` keyword.

But sometimes you don't want that behavior. In some situations, you might want other patterns in the `case` statement to be checked, or other actions taken. The syntax in bash allows for this, with `;;&` and `;&` used to indicate these variations.

Here's an example of that behavior that provides details about the path in $filename:

```
case $filename in
    ./*) echo -n "local "            # Begins with ./
        ;&                          # Fall through!
    [^/]*) echo -n "relative "      # Starts w/ anything but a slash
        ;;&                         # Look for other matches
    /*) echo -n "absolute "         # Begins with a slash
        ;&                          # Fall through
    */*) echo "pathname"            # A slash anywhere
        ;;                          # Done
    *) echo "filename"              # All other
        ;;                          # Done
esac
```

The patterns will be compared, in order, to the value in $filename. The first pattern is two literal characters—a period and a slash—followed by any characters. If that matches (e.g., if the value of $filename was ./this/file), then the script will print "local" but without the newline at the end. The next line is ;&, which tells bash to "fall through" and execute the command(s) associated with the next pattern (without even checking for a match). So it will also print "relative." Unlike the previous pattern, this section of code ends with ;;&, which tells bash to try other patterns (going forward, in order) for a match, too.

So now it will check the next pattern, looking for a leading slash. If that doesn't match, the next one might. It looks for a slash anywhere in the string (any—zero or more—characters, then a slash, then any characters). If that matches (and it would in our example), it will print the word pathname. The ;; indicates that no more patterns need to be examined, and it would be done.

Style and Readability: Recap

In this chapter, we described the case statement, an n-way branch in the flow of execution. Its pattern-matching feature makes it very useful in scripting, though a common use is a simple, literal match of particular words.

The variations ;;, ;;&, and ;& provide some useful functionality but can be tricky. It might be better to structure such logic using if/then/else rather than a case statement.

These symbols are so subtly different that it can be easy to overlook what happens at each step. The control flow after a match is made can be different for each case: to fall through executing more code, to try to match another pattern, or to be done. Therefore we strongly encourage you to comment on your choices in your scripts to avoid confusion or misunderstanding.

## CHAPTER 4

Variable Vernacular

It is not uncommon to see an error message or an assignment statement that contains the idiom ${0##*/}, which looks to be some sort of reference to $0, but something more is going on. Let's take a closer look at variable references and what some of these extra characters do for us. What we'll find is a whole array of string manipulations that give you quite a bit of power in a few special characters.

Variable Reference

Referencing a variable's value is very straightforward in most programming languages. You either just use the name of the variable or add a character to the name to explicitly say that you want to retrieve the value. That's true with bash: you assign to the variable by name, VAR=something, and you retrieve the value with a dollar-sign prefix: $VAR. If you're wondering why we need the dollar sign, consider that bash deals largely with strings, so:

```
MSG="Error: FILE not found"
```

will give you a simple literal string of the four words shown, whereas:

```
MSG="Error: $FILE not found"
```

will replace the $FILE with the value of that variable (which, presumably, would hold the name of the file that it was looking for).

Variable Interpolation

Be sure to use double quotes if you want this string substitution to occur. Using single quotes takes all characters literally, and no substitutions happen.

To avoid confusion over where the variable name ends (the spaces make it easy in this example), a more complete syntax for variable reference uses braces around the variable name ${FILE}, and could have been used in our example.

This syntax, with the braces, is the foundation for much special syntax around variable references. For example, we can put a hash sign in front of a variable name ${#VAR}, to return not its value but the string length of the value.

${VAR}	${#VAR}
oneword	7
/usr/bin/longpath.txt	21
many words in one string	24
3	1
2356	4
1427685	7

But bash can do more than simply retrieve the value or its length.

Parameter Expansion

When retrieving the value of a variable, certain substitutions or edits can be specified, affecting the value that is returned (though not the value in the variable—except in one case). The syntax involves special sequences of characters inside the braces used to delineate the variable's name, like the characters inside these braces: ${VAR##*/}. Here are a few such expansions worth knowing.

Shorthand for basename

When you invoke a script, you might use just its filename as the command to invoke the script, but that assumes that the script has execute permissions and is in a directory located in one of the directories in your PATH variable. You might invoke the script with ./*scriptname* if the script is in your current directory. You might invoke it with a full pathname, /home/smith/utilities/scriptname, or even a relative pathname if your current working directory is nearby.

Whichever way you invoke the script, $0 will contain the sequence of characters that you used to invoke the script—relative path or absolute path, however you expressed it.

When you want to print that script's name out in a usage message, you likely want just the basename, the name of the file itself, not any of the path that got you there:

```
echo "usage: ${0##*/} namesfile datafile"
```

You might see it in a usage message, telling the user the correct syntax for running the script, or it might be the righthand side of an assignment to a variable. In that later case, we hope that the variable is called something like PROGRAM or SCRIPT because that's what this expression returns—the name of the script that is executing.

Let's take a closer look at this particular parameter expansion on $0, one that you can use to get just the basename without all the other parts of the path.

Path or Prefix Removal

You can remove characters from the front (prefix or lefthand side) or the tail (suffix or righthand side) of that value. To remove a certain set of characters from the left side of a string, you add a # and a shell pattern onto the parameter reference, a pattern that matches those characters that you want to remove.

The expression ${MYVAL#img_} would remove the characters img_ if they were the first characters of the string in the MYVAL variable. Using a more complex pattern, we could write ${MYVAL#*_}. This would remove any sequence of characters up to, and including, an underscore. (If there was no such pattern that matched, its full value is returned unaltered.)

A single # says that it will use the *shortest* match possible (nongreedy). A double ## says to use the *longest* match possible (greedy).

Now, perhaps, can you see what the expression ${0##*/} will do?

It will start with the value in $0, the pathname used to invoke the script. Then, from the lefthand side of the value, it will remove the longest match of any number of characters ending in a slash. Thus, it is removing all the parts of the path used in invoking the script, leaving just the name of the script itself.

Here are some possible values for $0 and this pattern we've discussed, to see how both the short (#) and long (##) match might differ in results:

Value in $0	Expression	Result returned
./ascript	${0#*/}	ascript
./ascript	${0##*/}	ascript
../bin/ascript	${0#*/}	bin/ascript
../bin/ascript	${0##*/}	ascript
/home/guy/bin/ascript	${0#*/}	home/guy/bin/ascript
/home/guy/bin/ascript	${0##*/}	ascript

Notice that the shortest matching pattern for */ can match just the slash by itself.

Shell Patterns, Not Regular Expressions

The patterns used in parameter expansion are *not* regular expressions. They are only shell pattern matching, where * matches 0 or more characters, ? matches a single character, and [chars] matches any one of the characters inside the braces.

Shorthand for dirname or Suffix Removal

Similar to how # will remove a prefix, that is, remove from the lefthand side, we can remove a suffix, that is, from the righthand side, by using %. A double percent sign indicates removing the longest possible match. Here are some examples that show how to remove a suffix. The first examples show a variable $FN, which holds the name of an image file. It might end in .jpg or .jpeg or .png or .gif. See how the different patterns remove various parts of the righthand side of the string. The last few examples show how to get something similar to dirname from the $0 parameter:

Value in shell variable	Expression	Result returned
img.1231.jpg	${FN%.*}	img.1234
img.1231.jpg	${FN%%.*}	img
./ascript	${0%/*}	.
./ascript	${0%%/*}	.
/home/guy/bin/ascript	${0%/*}	/home/guy/bin
/home/guy/bin/ascript	${0%%/*}	

This parameter substitution for dirname isn't an exact replica of the output from the command. It differs in the case where the path is /file because dirname would return just a slash, whereas our parameter substitution would remove it all. You can check for this if you want with some additional logic in your script, you could ignore this case if you don't expect to see it, or you can just add a slash to the end of the parameter, as in ${0%/*}/, so that all results would end in a slash.

Prefix and Suffix Removal

You can remember that # removes the left part and % the right part because, at least on a standard US keyboard, # is shift-3, which is to the left of % at shift-5.

Other Modifiers

More than just # and %, there are a few other modifiers that can alter a value via parameter expansion. You can convert either the first character or all characters in a string to uppercase via ^ or ^^, respectively, or to lowercase via , or ,, as shown in these examples:

Value in shell variable TXT	Expression	Result returned
message to send	${TXT^}	Message to send
message to send	${TXT^^}	MESSAGE TO SEND
Some Words	${TXT,}	some Words
Do Not YELL	${TXT,,}	do not yell

You might also consider declare -u UPPER and declare -l lower, which declare these shell variables to have their content converted to upper- or lowercase, respectively, for any text assigned to those variables.

The most flexible modifier is the one that does a substitution anywhere in the string, not just at the front or tail of the string. Similar to the sed command, it uses the slash, /, to indicate what pattern to match and what value to replace it with. A single slash means a single substitution (of the first occurrence). Using two slashes means to replace every occurrence. Here are a few examples:

Value in shell variable FN	Expression	Result returned
FN="my filename with spaces.txt"	${FN/ /_}	my_filename with spaces.txt
FN="my filename with spaces.txt"	${FN// /_}	my_filename_with_spaces.txt
FN="my filename with spaces.txt"	${FN// /}	myfilenamewithspaces.txt
FN="/usr/bin/filename"	${FN//\// }	usr bin filename
FN="/usr/bin/filename"	${FN/\// }	usr/bin/filename

No Trailing Slash

Note that there is no trailing slash like you would find in other similar commands like sed or vi. The closing brace ends the substitution.

Why not always use this substitution mechanism? Why bother with # or % substitution from the ends of the string? Consider this filename: frank.gifford.gif, and suppose you wanted to change this filename to a jpg file using Image Magick's convert command (that's another story). The substitute using / doesn't have a way to anchor the search to one end of the string or the other. If you had read in the filename and tried to replace the .gif with .jpg, what you would end up with is frank.jpgford.gif. For situations like this, the % substitution, which takes from the end of the string, works much better.

Another useful modifier will extract a substring of the variable. After the variable name, put a colon, then the offset to the first character of the substring that you want to extract. Since this is an offset, start at 0 for the first character of the string. Next, put another colon and the length of the substring you want. If you leave off this second colon and a length, then you get the whole rest of the string. Here are a few examples:

Value in shell variable FN	Expression	Result returned
/home/bin/util.sh	${FN:0:1}	/
/home/bin/util.sh	${FN:1:1}	h
/home/bin/util.sh	${FN:3:2}	me
/home/bin/util.sh	${FN:10:4}	util
/home/bin/util.sh	${FN:10}	util.sh

Example 4-1 shows the use of parameter expansion to parse data out of some input to create and process specific fields to use when automatically creating a configuration for firewall rules. We've also included a larger table of bash *parameter expansions* in the code, as we do a lot in this book, as a "real code readability" example. The output follows in Example 4-2.

Example 4-1. Parsing using parameter expansions: code

```
#!/usr/bin/env bash
# parameter-expansion.sh: parameter expansion for parsing, and a big list
# Original Author & date: _bash Idioms_ 2022
# bash Idioms filename: examples/ch04/parameter-expansion.sh
#_____
# Does not work on Zsh 5.4.2!

customer_subnet_name='Acme Inc subnet 10.11.12.13/24'

echo ''
echo "Say we have this string: $customer_subnet_name"

customer_name=${customer_subnet_name%subnet*}     # Trim from 'subnet' to end
subnet=${customer_subnet_name##* }                # Remove leading 'space*'
ipa=${subnet%/*}                                  # Remove trailing '/*'
cidr=${subnet#*/}                                 # Remove up to '/*'
fw_object_name=${customer_subnet_name// /_}       # Replace space with '_-
fw_object_name=${fw_object_name////-}             # Replace '/' with '-'
fw_object_name=${fw_object_name,,}                # Lowercase

echo ''
echo 'When the code runs we get:'
echo ''
echo "Customer name: $customer_name"
echo "Subnet:        $subnet"
echo "IPA            $ipa"
echo "CIDR mask:     $cidr"
```

```
echo "FW Object:      $fw_object_name"

# bash Shell Parameter Expansion: https://oreil.ly/Af8lw

# ${var#pattern}                    Remove shortest (nongreedy) leading pattern
# ${var##pattern}                   Remove longest (greedy) leading pattern
# ${var%pattern}                    Remove shortest (nongreedy) trailing pattern
# ${var%%pattern}                   Remove longest (greedy) trailing pattern

# ${var/pattern/replacement}        Replace first +pattern+ with +replacement+
# ${var//pattern/replacement}       Replace all +pattern+ with +replacement+

# ${var^pattern}                    Uppercase first matching optional pattern
# ${var^^pattern}                   Uppercase all matching optional pattern
# ${var,pattern}                    Lowercase first matching optional pattern
# ${var,,pattern}                   Lowercase all matching optional pattern

# ${var:offset}                     Substring starting at +offset+
# ${var:offset:length}              Substring starting at +offset+ for +length+

# ${var:-default}                   Var if set, otherwise +default+
# ${var:-default}                   Assign +default+ to +var+ if +var+ not already set
# ${var:?error_message}             Barf with +error_message+ if +var+ not set
# ${var:+replaced}                  Expand to +replaced+ if +var+ _is_ set

# ${#var}                           Length of var
# ${!var[*]}                        Expand to indexes or keys
# ${!var[@]}                        Expand to indexes or keys, quoted

# ${!prefix*}                       Expand to variable names starting with +prefix+
# ${!prefix@}                       Expand to variable names starting with +prefix+, quoted

# ${var@Q}                          Quoted
# ${var@E}                          Expanded (better than `eval`!)
# ${var@P}                          Expanded as prompt
# ${var@A}                          Assign or declare
# ${var@a}                          Return attributes
```

Example 4-2. Parsing using parameter expansions: output

Say we have this string: Acme Inc subnet 10.11.12.13/24

When the code runs we get:

```
Customer name: Acme Inc
Subnet:        10.11.12.13/24
IPA            10.11.12.13
CIDR mask:     24
FW Object:     acme_inc_subnet_10.11.12.13-24
```

Conditional Substitutions

Some of these variable substitutions are conditional, that is, they happen only if certain conditions are met. You could accomplish the same thing using if statements around the assignments, but these idioms make for shorter code for certain common cases. These conditional substitutions are shown here with a colon and then another special character: a minus, plus, or equal sign. The condition that they check for is this: is the variable null or unset? A null variable is a variable whose value is the null string. An unset variable is one that hasn't yet been assigned or was explicitly unset (think "discarded") with the unset command. With positional parameters (like $1, $2, etc.), they are unset if the user doesn't supply a parameter in that position.

If you don't include the colon in these conditional substitutions, then they only consider the case of an unset variable; null values are returned as is.

Default Values

A common scenario is a script with a single, optional parameter. If the parameter isn't supplied when the script is invoked, then a default value should be used. In bash, we might write something like this:

```
LEN=${1:-5}
```

This will set the variable LEN either to the value of the first parameter ($1)—if one was supplied—or else to the value 5. Here is an example script:

```
LEN="${1:-5}"
cut -d',' -f2-3 /tmp/megaraid.out | sort | uniq -c | sort -rn | head -n "$LEN"
```

It takes the second and third fields from a comma-separated values file called /tmp/megaraid.out, sorts those values, provides a count of the number of occurrences of each value pair, then shows the top 5 from the list. You can override the default value of 5 and show the top 3 or 10 (or however many you want) simply by specifying that count as the sole parameter to the script.

Comma-Separated Lists

Another conditional substitution, using the plus sign, also checks to see if the variable has a value and if so, if it will return a different value. That is, it returns the specified different value only if the variable is not null. Yes, that does sound strange; if it has a value, why return a different value?

A handy use for this seemingly odd logic is to construct a comma-separated list. You typically construct such a list by repeatedly appending ",value" or "value," for every value. When doing so, you usually need an if statement to avoid having an extra comma on the front or end of this list—but not when you use this join idiom:

```
for fn in * ; do
    S=${LIST:+,}              # S for separator
    LIST="${LIST}${S}${fn}"
done
```

See also Example 7-1.

Modified Value

Up to now, none of these substitutions have modified the underlying value of the variable. There is, however, one that does. If we write ${VAR:=value}, it will act much like our preceding default value idiom, but with one big exception. If VAR is empty or unset, it will assign that value to the variable (hence, the equal sign) and return that value. (If VAR is already set, it will simply return its existing value.) Note, however, that this assigning of a value does *not* work for positional parameters (like $1), which is why you don't see it used nearly as often.

$RANDOM

Bash has a very handy $RANDOM variable. As the "Bash Variables" section in the Bash Reference Manual (*https://oreil.ly/aQSXr*) says:

> Each time this parameter is referenced, a random integer between 0 and 32767 is generated. Assigning a value to this variable seeds the random number generator.

While this is not suitable for cryptographic functions, it's useful for rolling the dice or adding a bit of noise into otherwise too-predictable operations. We use this later in "A Simple Word Count Example" on page 69.

As shown in Example 4-3, you can pick a random element out of a list.

Example 4-3. Pick a random list element

```
declare -a mylist
mylist=(foo bar baz one two "three four")

range=${#mylist[@]}
random=$(( $RANDOM % $range ))  # 0 to list length count

echo "range = $range, random = $random, choice = ${mylist[$random]}"

# Shorter but less readable 6 months from now:
# echo "choice = ${mylist[$(( $RANDOM % ${#mylist[@]} ))]}"
```

You may also see something like this:

```
TEMP_DIR="$TMP/myscript.$RANDOM"
[ -d "$TEMP_DIR" ] || mkdir "$TEMP_DIR"
```

However, that is subject to race conditions (*https://oreil.ly/Z5P8d*), and is obviously a simple pattern. It is also partly predictable, but sometimes you want to have a clue as to what code is cluttering up $TMP. Don't forget to set a trap (see "It's a Trap!" on page 97) to clean up after yourself. We recommend you consider using mktemp, though that's a large issue outside the scope of bash idioms.

$RANDOM and dash

$RANDOM is not available in *dash*, which is */bin/sh* in some Linux distributions. Notably, current versions of Debian and Ubuntu use *dash* because it is smaller and faster than bash and thus helps to boot faster. But that means that */bin/sh*, which used to be a symlink to bash, is now a symlink to *dash* instead, and various bash-specific features will not work. It does work in Zsh though.

Command Substitution

We've already used *command substitution* quite a bit in Chapter 2, but we haven't talked about it. The old Bourne way to do it is `` (backticks/backquotes), but we prefer the more readable POSIX (*https://oreil.ly/eRXrr*) $() instead. You will see a lot of both forms, because it's how you pull output into a variable; for example:

```
unique_lines_in_file="$(sort -u "$my_file" | wc -l)"
```

Note that these are the same, but the second one is internal and faster:

```
for arg in $(cat /some/file)
for arg in $(< /some/file)       # Faster than shelling out to cat
```

Command Substitution

Command substitution is critical to cloud and other DevOps automation because it allows you to gather and use all the IDs and details that only exist at runtime; for example:

```
instance_id=$(aws ec2 run-instances --image $base_ami_id ... \
  --output text --query 'Instances[*].InstanceId')

state=$(aws ec2 describe-instances --instance-ids $instance_id \
  --output text --query 'Reservations[*].Instances[*].State.Name')
```

Nesting Command Substitution

Nesting command substitution using `` ` `` gets very ugly, very fast, because you must escape the inner backticks in each nesting layer. It's much easier to use $( ) if you can, as shown:

```
### Just Works
$ echo $(echo $(echo $(echo inside)))
inside

### Broken
$ echo `echo `echo `echo inside```
echo inside

### "Works" but very ugly
$ echo `echo \`echo \\\`echo inside\\\`\``
inside
```

Thanks to our reviewer Ian Miell for pointing this out and providing the example.

Style and Readability: Recap

When referencing a variable in bash, you have the opportunity to edit the value as you set or retrieve it. A few special characters at the end of the variable reference can remove characters from the front or end of the string value, alter its characters to upper- or lowercase, substitute characters, or give you just a substring of the original value. Common use of these handy features results in idioms for default values, basename and dirname substitutes, and the creation of a comma-separated list without using an explicit if statement.

Variable substitutions are a great feature in bash, and we recommend making good use of them. However, we also strongly recommend that you comment those statements to make it clear what sort of substitution you are attempting. The next reader of your code will thank you.

Expressions and Arithmetic

Bash offers many different ways to do the same thing—and some almost-identical syntax to do very different things. Often, it's just the difference of a few special characters. We've already seen ${VAR} and ${#VAR}, where the first expression returns the value of the variable but the second returns its string length ("Variable Reference" on page 31). Or ${VAR[@]} and ${VAR[*]} with their quoting differences ("Quotes and Spaces" on page 14).

Other bash idioms might make you wonder: when should you use two or just one set of square brackets? Or even none? What, if any, is the difference between ((...)) and $((...)) ? Usually there is some common meaning in the symbols across their various uses that hints at some semblance of reason behind the syntax. Sometimes the choice of expression was more for historical reasons. Let's take a look and see if we can explain some of these idiomatic pattern and arithmetic expressions.

Integer Only

The bash shell uses only integer arithmetic. Its main purpose is for counting things: iterations, numbers of files, sizes in bytes. What if you want or need a floating point calculation? After all, the sleep command now allows a fractional value: sleep 0.25 will sleep for a quarter of a second. What if you want to sleep multiples of a quarter of a second? You'd like to write sleep $((6 * 0.25)), but that won't work.

The easiest solution is to do the calculation using another program like bc or awk. For example, here's a script called fp that you could put in your ~/bin directory or somewhere else on your PATH (and give it execute permissions):

```
# /bin/bash -
# fp - provide floating point, via awk
# usage:  fp  "expression"

awk "BEGIN { print $* }"
```

With that in place, you could then write sleep $(fp "6 * 0.25") to get the desired floating point calculation. It may not be bash doing the calculation, but it is bash helping you get the calculation done.

Arithmetic

Although bash is largely a string-oriented language, whenever you see double parentheses in bash, it means that arithmetic evaluation is going on—arithmetic with integers, not strings. This is familiar to you from the for loop variation that uses double parens:

```
for ((i=0; i<size; i++))
```

Notice that we don't have to use the $ in front of variable names inside the double parens. That is true whenever we use double parens in bash. So where else do we find double parens in use?

First, we can use a dollar sign and double parens to do an arithmetic calculation to create a value for a shell variable, like these:

```
max=$(( intro + body + outro - 1 ))
median_loc=$((len / 2))
```

Again, notice that the variables don't need the dollar sign reference in front of them when they are used inside of double parens.

Second, consider this use of double parens:

```
if (( max - 3 > x * 4 )) ; then
    # Do something here
fi
```

This time we are using double parens without a leading dollar sign. Why? What's different?

In the first case, for variable assignments, we want the value of the expression, so just like with variables, the dollar sign indicates that we want the value. In the second case, an if statement, we don't use the dollar sign because we only need the true/false Boolean value to make our decision. If the expression inside the double parens (without a dollar sign) is a nonzero value, then the return status of the parenthesized expression is 0—which is considered "true" in bash. Otherwise, the return status is 1 (which, in bash, is "false").

Notice that we said "return status?" That's because the double parens with no dollar sign is used, syntactically, as if you were executing one or more commands. It doesn't return a value that you could use to assign to a variable. However, you can use it to assign a new value to a variable in certain cases since bash supports some C language-style assignment operators. Here are a few examples. These are complete bash statements, one per line:

```
(( step++ ))
(( median_loc = len / 2 ))
(( dist *= 4 ))
```

Each statement is performing an arithmetic evaluation, but in each case, there is an assignment of a value that also occurs as part of that evaluation. No value is returned from the expression, only the return status—which you could examine in the $? variable after each statement executes.

Could you write those three calculations from the preceding example using the dollar-sign-double-paren syntax? It may look more familiar to write:

```
step=$(( step + 1 ))
median_loc=$(( len / 2 ))
dist=$(( dist * 4 ))
```

We don't want to write $((step++)) on a line by itself because that expression will return a numeric value—which the shell will then take as the name of a command to be executed. If step++ evaluated to 3, the shell would subsequently look for a command named 3.

A Reminder About Spaces

In a bash variable assignment, *no* spaces are allowed around the equals sign. For variable assignment, syntactically, it all must be one "word" of text. However, inside the parentheses, spaces are OK since the parens define the boundary for that "word."

Now there is just one more arithmetic variation—probably for historical reasons. You can use the shell builtin `let` to act like the double parens without the dollar sign. So compare these equivalent statements:

```
(( step++ ))    # Is the same as:
let "step++"

(( median_loc = len / 2 ))  # Is the same as:
let "median_loc = len / 2"

(( dist *= 4 ))    # Is the same as:
let "dist*=4"
```

But be careful—if you don't use quotes (single or double) around the `let` expression, then you better not have any spaces in that expression at all. (The first `let` in our example doesn't need the quotes, but it's a good habit to always use them.) Spaces will divide your command into separate words, and `let` only takes a single word, so you'll get a syntax error if there is more than one word.

No Parentheses Needed

We said that bash is a string-oriented language, but there is a way to make an exception. You can declare a variable as an integer like this: `declare -i MYVAR`, and having done so, you can do arithmetic to assign it a value without using double parentheses and without the $ in front of variable names. Here's an example, a script `seesaw.sh`:

```
declare -i SEE
X=9
Y=3
SEE=X+Y          # Only this one will be arithmetic
SAW=X+Y          # This is just a literal string
SUM=$X+$Y        # This is string concatenation
echo "SEE = $SEE"
echo "SAW = $SAW"
echo "SUM = $SUM"
```

What you get if you run these statements shows how bash is mostly string oriented. The values of SAW and SUM are formed by string operations. Only SEE is given its value by doing arithmetic:

```
$ bash seesaw.sh
SEE = 12
SAW = X+Y
SUM = 9+3
$
```

This shows that you can do arithmetic without the need for double parentheses—but we usually avoid this, as it requires that you declare as an integer the variable to which you are assigning things. If you forget the declare statement or if you assign such an expression to a variable not so declared, you won't get any error message—just an unwanted result.

Compound Commands

You are probably very familiar with seeing a single command on a line by itself in a script. You may also be familiar with using a single command in an if statement's condition to see if the command succeeded, and taking action depending on the result. If you've read Chapter 1, you've seen the "no-if" if statement idiom, too. Now let's take a look at the simple one-command if statement, one that looks like this:

```
if cd $DIR ; then # Do something ...
```

But what about these:

```
if [ $DIR ]; then # Do something ...
if [[ $DIR ]]; then # Do something ...
```

Why the brackets in these two lines and not in the first example? Is there a difference? What about one versus two brackets; which should you use and when/why?

Without any brackets, what is happening is the execution of a command (cd in our example). The success or failure of that command is returned as, in effect, a true or false for the if to use in its decision branching between the then or the else (should there be one). In bash, you can put an entire pipeline of commands (e.g., cmd | sort | wc) in an if statement. It is the return status of the last command in the pipeline that determines whether the if statement is true or false. (And that can mask errors that are very hard to find; see set -o pipefail in "Unofficial bash Strict Mode" on page 96.)

The single bracket syntax is actually also running a command, the shell builtin test command. The single left bracket is a shell builtin for the same thing, the test command, but with one difference: a required final argument of]. The double-bracket syntax is, technically, a bash keyword, one that indicates a compound command, whose behavior is very similar, though not identical, to the single bracket and test command.

We use either single- or double-bracket syntax to do some logic and comparisons, that is, conditional expressions. We use them for checking the state of things, like if a file exists or has certain permissions, or if a shell variable has a value or not. See the bash man page under "Conditional Expressions" (*https://oreil.ly/Bn5gv*) for a full list of the tests and checks you can make, and `help test` for quick reminders.

Our preceding example is checking to see if the DIR variable has a non-null value. Another way to write this would be:

```
if [[ -n "$DIR" ]]; then ...
```

to see if the value is not null, that is, has a nonzero length. Conversely, to see if the variable's value is zero length, i.e., unset or null, use:

```
if [[ -z "$DIR" ]]; then ...
```

So are there differences between the single- and double-bracket tests? Just a few, but they can be significant.

Perhaps the biggest difference is that the double-bracket syntax supports an additional comparison operator, =~, which allows the use of regular expressions:

```
if [[ "$FILE_NAME" =~ .*xyzz*.*jpg ]]; then ...
```

Regular Expressions

This is the *one and only* place in bash where you will find regular expressions! And remember: do *not* put your regular expression in quotes or you will be matching those characters verbatim and not as a regular expression.

Another difference between single and double brackets is more stylistic, but one that will affect portability. These two forms do the same thing:

```
if [[ $VAR == "literal" ]]; then ...
```

```
if [ $VAR = "literal" ]; then ...
```

The use of the single equals sign for comparison may seem unnatural for C and Java programmers, but when used in bash conditional expressions, both = and == mean the same thing. The single equals sign is preferred in the single bracket syntax for POSIX compliance (so says the bash man page).

A Subtle Sort of Difference

Within the double square brackets, the < and > operators compare "lexicographically using the current locale," whereas test (and [ ) compare using simple ASCII ordering.

You will also likely need to escape these operators (like this: if [$x \> $y]) when using single brackets, otherwise they will be taken to mean redirection. Why? Because the single bracket, like the test command, is a builtin command not a keyword, so bash sees it as running a command—and you can redirect I/O when running a command. However, when bash sees the double brackets, a keyword, it knows to expect such operators and doesn't treat them as redirection. Therefore, of the two syntax forms, we much prefer the double-bracket syntax.

Both single- and double-bracket expressions can use an older, more Fortran-like syntax for their numeric comparisons. For example, they use -le for less-than-or-equal-to comparison. Here's where another difference between the two arises. The arguments to either side of this operator must be simple integers in the single bracket expression. Using double brackets, each operand can be a larger arithmetic expression, though without spaces unless quoted. For example:

```
if [[ $OTHERVAL*10 -le $VAL/5 ]] ; then ...
```

A better choice if you're doing arithmetic expressions and comparisons is to use the double-parentheses syntax. That gives you the more familiar C/Java/Python-like comparison operators and more freedom regarding spacing:

```
if (( OTHERVAL * 10 <= VAL / 5 )) ; then ...
```

Style and Readability: Recap

With so many variations to choose from, which if statement style do you choose? We choose the style that best fits the calculation under consideration.

When it is a mathematical expression, we use the double parentheses. As a rule, in bash, double parens indicate arithmetic is going on. The dollar sign indicates that you want the value of the expression returned, otherwise you just get a success/fail result status. But operator-rich bash makes it possible to do similar things using either the double-paren syntax or the let builtin. Since the $ isn't needed on variables to get their values inside double parentheses, we try to omit them consistently.

For arithmetic expressions, some people may prefer the double parentheses around the expression, consistent with the if statements. However, for others the simple let builtin command reads cleanly and simply. You can live dangerously and skip the double parens by declaring your variables as integers, but we cannot recommend that. It is too easy to mix and match variables, some of which may not have been declared as integers. Confusion ensues. Putting the expression in double parentheses (or using let) guarantees that it will remain an arithmetic evaluation.

For text-heavy comparisons, we use the double brackets, especially because that lets us use regular expressions.

For conditionals, the newer syntax of [[is much preferred over [. However, if your conditional is arithmetic comparisons, an even better choice is the ((syntax.

Functional Framework

The two preceding chapters have described the bash idioms in using variables and then combining those variables into expressions. The next level up is grouping those expressions and statements into functions that can be called from various locations within a bash shell script. Even though bash does support the useful construct of functions, it does so in a very bashy way. Let's see how it differs from what you know from other languages.

Calling Functions

Here are three statements that are examples of calling bash functions (which we are making up for this example):

```
Do_Something
Find_File  25 $MPATH $ECODE
Show_All $*
```

Those don't look like function calls, you might be thinking. They look just like any command line invocation of a command.

Exactly.

In other languages, you might say something like Find_File(25, MPATH, ECODE), but that is not bash. In bash, a function is called much like any command; you invoke it like you would invoke a command or a shell script. As with a bash keyword or builtin, the shell doesn't need to create a separate process to run the function. That makes a function more efficient than calling a separate command binary or shell script.

You might also notice that these function calls are not returning a value that can be assigned to another variable. More on that in the following sections. First, let's look at how we define functions and their parameters.

Defining Functions

The syntax for bash includes some optional elements. Let's say, for example, that you want to define a function called helper. Here are three different ways to begin that definition:

```
function Helper ()
function Helper
Helper ()
```

All three are equivalent. The reserved word function is optional, but if you do use it, then the parentheses are optional. We prefer to use the simple two-word version: function and then the name of our function. Not only does it clearly state what we're doing, but it reminds us that, unlike other languages, our functions parameters are not put in parentheses. And it's quite easy to grep for.

The body of the function follows this defining of the function's name, usually enclosed in braces:

```
function Say_So {
    echo 'Here we are in the function named Say_So'
}
```

Function Parameters

How are parameters defined for a bash function? They are not. Instead, when you call a bash function (described in the following paragraphs), you can supply as many parameters as you want. Typically you have a certain fixed set of parameters in mind and will write your function accordingly, but there's nothing special that you would need to do to have a variable number of arguments.

The arguments, however many are provided, are available to the function as $1 , $2, $3, and so forth, using the same syntax used for parameters to the bash script itself. Since these parameters don't have names but only their order number, it is a very good idea to put a comment at the head of the function to document what parameters the function expects and in what order. It is also quite common to see, in the first few lines of a script, that these positional parameters are assigned to variables with more descriptive names.

Since the function's parameters are using the $1, etc., names, you may be wondering what happens to the shell script's parameters that are referenced using that same syntax. Calling the function doesn't change the script's parameters; the script's parameters simply are not visible inside the function (unless, of course, you send them in as parameters to the function).

There is one exception, however. The $0 parameter, the one that holds the name of the script, is still there and still holds the name of the script, however it was invoked. You can still find the name of the function, though. There is an array variable named FUNCNAME that holds the call stack of the functions that have been invoked. Element 0 is always the current function, so just use $FUNCNAME (since using the array name without an index always returns the first element, i.e., the one at index zero). That's useful in a debugging prompt; see Example 10-3.

The following function will echo out the two parameters passed in to the function:

```
function See2it {
    echo "First arg: $1"
    echo "Second arg: $2"
}
```

If insufficient arguments are supplied in calling the function, the corresponding parameters are null.

This is a simple example of echoing the parameters with which the function is called:

```
function Tell_All {
    echo "You called $FUNCNAME"
    echo "The $# args supplied are:"
    for arg in "$@"; do
        echo "$arg"
    done
}

Tell_All 47 tree /tmp
```

When that script is run, here is what the output looks like:

```
You called Tell_All
The 3 args supplied are:
47
tree
/tmp
```

Function Return Values

Here, too, bash functions are more like scripts than they are like your typical computer language functions. The return value from bash functions is really just an exit status, the value that you can check using $? after calling the function. Just as you might check $? after calling another script or an executable, so, too, does a bash function indicate the success or failure of the function. It actually returns the exit status of the last command executed in the function.

So how is the script writer supposed to get any useful results back from a bash function? There are two typical approaches. One way is to treat the function just like you would any shell script—have its output be the return values. You might pipe that output into the next part of your script that needs the results from the function, or you might capture that output using $() notation. The $() will run the function in a subshell and you can assign the result (the function's output) to a variable, and then use that variable on another command line.

Another way to return results from a function in a shell script is to use something not available to an external script—global variables.

Local Variables

Consider a function that has some looping inside it, done by using a for loop, and that for loop uses an index variable i to count the iterations. Now consider what would happen if the function itself were called from within the body of a for loop, a loop that also happened to be controlled using i as an index variable. Since bash variables are global, then the (inner) function will affect the outer loop index. Not good. What to do?

Bash provides a syntax to let you declare variables as "local" so that they are not seen outside the function. Variables like i in a for loop should be declared as local variables:

```
function Summer {
    local i
    SUM=0
    for((i=0; i<$1; i++)) {
        let SUM+=i;
    }
}
```

Problem solved. It might be even better to use local -i i or declare -i i to declare i as an integer value, avoiding conversions to/from string. The declare inside a function acts just like the local in hiding any global variable by that name. The use of the -i option (in either case) allows you to specify the integer aspect of the variable.

The variable SUM in this example is not declared local because that is how the result of the function call is being returned to the caller. Should all variables in a function be declared local unless they are needed outside the script? Quite possibly, but since there is no way to enforce it, few programmers are that thorough. If you are writing functions that you expect to be shared and portable, then it is well worth the effort and will avoid unexpected side effects.

Dynamic Scoping

If you declare a local variable in a function and then that function calls another function, the second function will see the first function's local variable and *not* the global variable of the same name. If you call that second function from the main part of your script, it will see (and use) the global variable. Welcome to the dangers of dynamic scoping, another reason to keep your scripts simple and well documented.

Function Special Cases

Remember that the function definition must occur before it is called.

If you use parentheses in your function definition (unlike our preferred style), then you can enclose your function body in any of the compound statement syntax choices. You can use double parens for an arithmetic evaluation or double brackets if you want your function to do just a conditional expression evaluation. But these uses are highly unlikely.

You can put an I/O redirection on your function definition. It takes effect when you call that function. Here's a common use of that feature to easily redirect the entire usage message to STDERR (via 1>&2):

```
function Usage_Message {
    echo "usage:  $0  value pathname"
    echo "where value must be positive"
    echo "and pathname must be an existing file"
    echo "for example:  $0 25 /tmp/scratch.csv"
} 1>&2
```

This function might be called when the script checks and finds that the correct number of arguments have not been supplied or that the supplied filename doesn't exist (we'll talk about that more in "HELP!" on page 79). The important thing to note is that the output gets redirected to STDERR, but the redirection doesn't have to be put on every line of the script—only once, outside the enclosing braces. That can save you a lot of typing, *and* you don't need to remember to add another redirect to any lines when you revise the script.

Note that for the sake of clarity and easing into it, we've broken down some of our style recommendations for functions; see "Functions" on page 128 for details.

Time for printf

If you know `printf` from languages like C and Java, you've got a head start. We thought we'd cover it in this chapter on functions because, while not a function in bash but a builtin, it feels familiar enough to treat it like one.

Print formatted, or `printf`, is underutilized in bash since most people just use `echo`, but the bash builtin has a few idiomatic extensions that you'll want to be able to read and write. It is also defined in POSIX, unlike the bash builtin version of `echo`, so it is more portable if your script runs on non-Linux systems.

We're only going to talk about the bash builtin version, but you probably have an external binary that is not connected to bash and will not have the same options:

```
$ type -a printf
printf is a shell builtin
printf is /usr/bin/printf
```

The bash `printf` will be used unless you use the full path (`/usr/bin/printf`) or prefix it with env. Compare `printf --help` and `env printf --help` to see the differences.

We're also not going to go into a long list of standard `printf` formats; those are covered in many other places, including Appendix A of *bash Cookbook*.

For more details on your `printf` versions, see:

- `help printf` or `printf --help`
- `man 1 printf`
- Possibly `/usr/bin/printf --help` or `env printf --help`

POSIX Output

If your script will run on operating systems other than Linux, you should consider using `printf` instead of `echo` for consistency. It's simple but involves more typing than using `echo`, and unlike `echo`, does not automatically include a trailing newline:

```
printf '%s\n'    # Simple string, newline NOT automatically included
printf '%b\n'    # Also expand escape characters
```

You can use either single or double quotes around the `printf` format, and those quotes will follow the usual variable interpolation rules (single will not interpolate; double will), but escapes like \n will work inside both types of quotes. As we discuss elsewhere, we prefer single quotes to show programmer intent and prevent interpolation, unless you need to interpolate a variable inside the format, which may indicate you are doing something wrong.

For much more on this topic, see:

- *https://unix.stackexchange.com/a/65819*
- *https://www.in-ulm.de/~mascheck/various/echo+printf*

Getting or Using the Date and Time

Bash 4.2 added printf %(datefmt)T, but the default output was the Unix Epoch (*https://oreil.ly/gF7tQ*) (1970-01-01 00:00:00 -0000), which is probably not what you wanted. The default changed to "now" in bash 4.3, which makes more sense. There are two special arguments, -1, which means "now," and "-2," which means "the time the shell was invoked." You can provide an optional Epoch seconds time integer to display some other time, which is handy for translating Epoch seconds to human-readable time. We recommend using -1 for consistency and clarity of intent if you mean "now":

```
### Set a $today variable using -v
$ printf -v today '%(%F)T' '-1'
$ echo $today
2021-08-13

### Trivial logging (these are the same)
$ printf '%(%Y-%m-%d %H:%M:%S %z)T: %s\n' '-1' 'Your log message here'
$ printf '%(%F %T %z)T: %s\n' '-1' 'Your log message here'
2021-08-13 12:48:33 -0400: Your log message here

### When was 1628873101?
$ printf '%(%F %T)T = %s\n' '1628873101' 'Epoch 1628873101 to human readable'
2021-08-13 12:45:01 = Epoch 1628873101 to human readable
```

printf into a Variable

If you looked at help printf you may have noticed the -v var option, which assigns the output into a variable rather than displaying it, similar to sprintf in C. We'll see a use for that next.

For more details on this topic, see "Using logger from bash" on page 111.

We much prefer the bash builtin printf, but one thing the GNU[1] version of date still does better than printf %(datefmt)T is showing dates for other times, like date -d '2 months ago' '+%B', which tells us the name of the month from two months ago, like:

```
$ date -d '2 months ago' '+%B'
August
```

---

1 GNU (*https://oreil.ly/eG6nV*) is a recursive acronym that stands for "GNU's Not Unix."

Default bash on Mac Is Too Old

Note that `printf %(datefmt)T` requires at least bash 4.2, 4.3+ preferred, so this won't work in the older, but otherwise quite useful, default bash 3.2 on a Mac! See "bash on Mac" on page ix.

printf for Reuse or Debugging

Bash help says "%q quote the argument in a way that can be reused as shell input," and we will use that in Chapter 7 to show "shell *quoted*" strings, but here's a simple example:

```
$ printf '%q' "This example is from $today\n"
This\ example\ is\ from\ 2021-08-13\\n
```

This can be useful for reusing output elsewhere, creating formatted output (see also "Comma-Separated Lists" on page 38), and debugging where you need to be able to see hidden or control characters or fields. See also "bash Debugging" on page 120.

Style and Readability: Recap

Functions in bash are very much like internal shell scripts. Their invocation is very much like running any command, and their parameters are referenced like any shell script's parameters ($1, $2, etc.) You will need to put your functions at the front of the script so that their definition is seen before any call to the function. As in any language, functions should be kept short and be largely single-purpose. Using a single I/O redirection on a function can help you avoid repetitive redirections. Perhaps the biggest danger with functions is the variable references. Functions can return values via variables or by writing to STDOUT and having the caller pipe the function's output into some next command. You may need to refer to (global) variables to return values from a function, but there are some variables you want to avoid altering. Using `local` can help with that, but beware of dynamic typing—those local variables don't stay local if you call another function. Be sure to document this sort of thing in the function's opening comments.

The `printf` builtin behaves much like the familiar function from other languages. In addition to the standard formats, bash's `printf` has some useful idiomatic extensions. We especially appreciate not having to create a subshell to run the `date` command just to find out what time it is, especially if you are calling it frequently for logging.

List and Hash Handling

Computers, as we know, are very good at counting and organizing data. We can use code to count and organize data by using a *data structure*, and the building blocks for those are *arrays*. Bash has had arrays since the beginning and added *associative arrays* in version 4.0. You will run into hard-to-read code for bash arrays out there, partly because bash has a lot of history and backward compatibility to maintain, as we mentioned earlier, but also because some developers tend to overcomplicate things. Arrays are actually not that hard to implement, and you can write about them clearly with a little thought.

As a refresher, in computer science and programming, arrays are variables containing multiple elements that are indexed or referred to by an integer. Or in other words, an array is a variable containing a list instead of a scalar or single value. An associative array is a type of list that is indexed by a string instead of an integer. So it's a list of key-value pairs, that basically forms a dictionary or look-up table, where internally the key is hashed to form a memory location. More or less.

The bash documentation uses the terms *array* and *associative arrays*, but depending on your background, *lists* and *hashes*, or possibly *dictionaries* or *dicts*, may be more familiar, and they are certainly easier to type and say. The bash documentation also uses *subscript* where other people might say *index*. We usually follow the bash docs for consistency, but for these we're going to use the more common and understandable *list*, *hash*, and *subscript* terms.

Even though lists (arrays) came first, hashes (associative arrays) are slightly simpler because there is never any question about supplying the index (subscript), because it's required. The integer index of a list may be implied, and while it's not really complicated, there are operations that work for them that make no sense for a hash.

As the bash reference says, "Bash provides one-dimensional indexed and associative array variables." While it's possible to create really ugly multidimensional structures, doing so in bash will probably end in tears. If you really need to do that, consider doing it in a different language.

Watch Out for bash Versions with Hashes

You really need to be careful about your bash version here. As we just said, bash didn't get hashes (i.e., associative arrays) until version 4.0, and it took a couple of versions to sort out some details, like allowing $list[-1] to refer to the last integer element (v4.3), instead of needing $mylist[${#mylist[*]}-1] (where ${#mylist[*]} is the element count). Ouch.

As we said in "bash on Mac" on page ix, watch out for stock bash on a Mac; it's quite old. You'll find newer versions in MacPorts, Homebrew, or Fink.

Not POSIX

Also, arrays (lists and hashes) are not specified by POSIX, so if portability beyond bash is a concern, you'll need to be very careful using them because they might not work. For example, the Zsh syntax is a bit different, so these examples won't work on that on a Mac either.

Commonalities

Lists and hashes are very similar in bash, so we're going to start with what they have in common, then get to where they are different. In fact, you can treat lists as a subset of hashes that simply happen to have ordered integer indexes. We don't think you *should* do that, but you *can*.

Lists are inherently ordered, whereas hashes are inherently unordered, so there are operations like shift or push that only make sense for an ordered list. On the other hand, you would never need to sort the keys in an ordered list, but you might for a hash.

Accidental Assignment

An accidental assignment without a *subscript* will affect element zero, so myarray=*foo* results in creating or overwriting $myarray[0] with foo, even if it's a hash!

From the bash docs:

> If the subscript is @ or *, the word expands to all members of the array name. These subscripts differ only when the word appears within double quotes. If the word is double-quoted, "${name[*]}" expands to a single word with the value of each array member separated by the first character of the IFS variable (see "Fiddling with $IFS for Fun and Profit, to Read Files" on page 89), whereas "${name[@]}" expands each element of name to a separate word.

That's a mouthful isn't it? We've already talked about that in "Quotes and Spaces" on page 14, but it's important because, as we'll show, if you get it wrong you can hurt yourself. We've used printf "%q" with a pipe (|) delimiter in Example 7-1 to show "shell *quoted*" strings (technically "words") in a way that is visible in the output on the screen or on this page. The quoting rules are actually the same as we cover in Chapter 2, just in the context of a list or hash.

Lists

As we said, arrays, also known as *lists*, are variables containing multiple elements that are indexed or referred to by an integer.

In bash they start from zero and may be declared using declare -a, local -a, readonly -a, or by just assigning to a new variable like mylist[0]=foo or mylist=() (empty list). Once a variable is declared as a list, a simple assignment like mylist+=(bar) is the same as a *push*, which adds an item to the end of the list, but note the + and (), both of which are critical. See Table 7-1 for an example.

Table 7-1. Sample bash list

Element	Value
mylist[0]	foo
mylist[1]	bar
mylist[2]	baz

The common operations on an array or list are:

- Declare a variable as a list
- Assign one or more values to it
- If treating it as a stack (think plates in a cafeteria; FIFO: first on, first off, or first in, first out):

  — push

  — pop
- Display (dump) all values for debugging or reuse

- Reference one or all values (for, or for each)
- Reference a subset (slice) of values
- Delete one or more values
- Delete the entire list

Rather than talk about all of that, we're going to show you instead, and you can just pick out the idioms you need when you need them (Example 7-1).

Example 7-1. bash list example: code

```
#!/usr/bin/env bash
# lists.sh: bash list example code
# Original Author & date: _bash Idioms_ 2022
# bash Idioms filename: examples/ch07/lists.sh
#_____
# Does not work on Zsh 5.4.2!

# Books are not as wide as some screens!
FORMAT='fmt --width 70 --split-only'

# Declare a list                                              ❶
# declare -a mylist    # Can do this, or `local -a` or `readonly -a` or:
mylist[0]='foo'        # This both declares and assigns to mylist[0]

# OR Both declares & assigns:
#mylist=(foo bar baz three four "five by five" six)

# Push or assign, note the += and ()                          ❷
###mylist=(bar)                 # Would overwrite mylist[0]
mylist+=(bar)            # mylist[1]
mylist+=(baz)            # mylist[2]
mylist+=(three four)    # mylist[3] AND mylist[4]
mylist+=("five by five") # mylist[5] Note spaces and quotes
mylist+=("six")         # mylist[6]

# OR APPEND, note the "+" and we're assuming foo was already assigned
#mylist+=(bar baz three four "five by five" six)

# Display or dump the values                                  ❸
echo -e "\nThe element count is: ${#mylist[@]} or ${#mylist[*]}"

echo -e "\nThe length of element [4] is: ${#mylist[4]}"

echo -e "\nDump or list:"
declare -p mylist | $FORMAT
echo -n      "\${mylist[@]}  = " ; printf "%q|"  ${mylist[@]}
echo -en    "\n\${mylist[*]}  = " ; printf "%q|"  ${mylist[*]}
echo -en "\n\"\${mylist[@]}\" = " ; printf "%q|" "${mylist[@]}"
echo -en "\n\"\${mylist[*]}\" = " ; printf "%q|" "${mylist[*]}"
```

```bash
echo -e "    # Broken!"  # Previous line is bad and no newline
# See `help printf` or chapter 6 "printf for reuse or debugging", we need
# this to show the correct words:
# %q    quote the argument in a way that can be reused as shell input

# "Join" the values                                                    ❹
function Join { local IFS="$1"; shift; echo "$*"; } # One character delimiter!
# Note that the Join above requires "$*" and not "$@"!
echo -en "\nJoin ',' \${mylist[@]} = "; Join ',' "${mylist[@]}"
function String_Join {
    local delimiter="$1"
    local first_element="$2"
    shift 2
    printf '%s' "$first_element" "${@/#/$delimiter}"
    # Print first element, then reuse the '%s' format to display the rest of
    # the elements (from the function args $@), but add a prefix of $delimiter
    # by "replacing" the leading empty pattern (/#) with $delimiter.
}
echo -n "String_Join '<>' \${mylist[@]} = " ; String_Join '<>' "${mylist[@]}"

# Iterate over the values                                              ❺
echo -e "\nforeach \"\${!mylist[@]}\":"
for element in "${!mylist[@]}"; do
    echo -e "\tElement: $element; value: ${mylist[$element]}"
done

echo -e "\nBut don't do this: \${mylist[*]}"
for element in ${mylist[*]}; do
    echo -e "\tElement: $element; value: ${mylist[$element]}"
done

# Handle slices (subsets) of the list, shift and pop                   ❻
echo -e "\nStart from element 5 and show a slice of 2 elements:"
printf "%q|" "${mylist[@]:5:2}"
echo '' # No newline in above

echo -e "\nShift FIRST element [0] (dumped before and after):"
declare -p mylist | $FORMAT              # Display before
mylist=("${mylist[@]:1}")               # First element, needs quotes
#mylist=("${mylist[@]:$count}")         # First #count elements
declare -p mylist  | $FORMAT            # Display after

echo -e "\nPop LAST element (dumped before and after):"
declare -p mylist | $FORMAT
unset -v 'mylist[-1]'                   # bash v4.3+
#unset -v "mylist[${#mylist[*]}-1]"   # Older
declare -p mylist

# Delete slices                                                        ❼
echo -e "\nDelete element 2 using unset (dumped before and after):"
declare -p mylist
unset -v 'mylist[2]'
```

```
declare -p mylist

# Delete the entire list
unset -v mylist
```

❽

❶ Declare a variable as an array (we say that instead of *list* here because the flag is `-a`).

❷ Assign one or more values to it.

❸ Display (dump) all values for debugging or reuse; see Example 4-1.

❹ Two different `join` functions; see also "Comma-Separated Lists" on page 38.

❺ Iterate over the values; see Example 4-1.

❻ Handle slices (subsets) of the list, shift and pop.

❼ Delete slices.

❽ Delete the entire list. Beware of `unset` because there's a subtle catch. If you happen to have a file with the same name as a variable, globbing[1] can hurt you, and you can clobber[2] unexpected things. To avoid that, it's best to quote your variable. It's even safer to use `-v` to force `unset` to treat your argument as a shell variable, like `unset -v 'list'`.

It looks like Example 7-2 when you run it.

Example 7-2. bash list example: output

```
The element count is: 7 or 7

The length of element [4] is: 4

Dump or list:
declare -a mylist=([0]="foo" [1]="bar" [2]="baz" [3]="three"
[4]="four" [5]="five by five" [6]="six")
${mylist[@]}   = foo|bar|baz|three|four|five|by|five|six|
${mylist[*]}   = foo|bar|baz|three|four|five|by|five|six|
"${mylist[@]}" = foo|bar|baz|three|four|five\ by\ five|six|
"${mylist[*]}" = foo\ bar\ baz\ three\ four\ five\ by\ five\ six|    # Broken!

Join ',' ${mylist[@]} = foo,bar,baz,three,four,five by five,six
```

---

1 Interpolating and expanding wildcard patterns; see *https://oreil.ly/0gNay*.

2 Accidentally overwriting; see *https://oreil.ly/xEZhz*.

```
String_Join '<>' ${mylist[@]} = foo<>bar<>baz<>three<>four<>five by five<>six
foreach "${!mylist[@]}":
        Element: 0; value: foo
        Element: 1; value: bar
        Element: 2; value: baz
        Element: 3; value: three
        Element: 4; value: four
        Element: 5; value: five by five
        Element: 6; value: six

But don't do this: ${mylist[*]}
        Element: foo; value: foo
        Element: bar; value: foo
        Element: baz; value: foo
        Element: three; value: foo
        Element: four; value: foo
        Element: five; value: foo
        Element: by; value: foo
        Element: five; value: foo
        Element: six; value: foo

Start from element 5 and show a slice of 2 elements:
five\ by\ five|six|

Shift FIRST element [0] (dumped before and after):
declare -a mylist=([0]="foo" [1]="bar" [2]="baz" [3]="three"
[4]="four" [5]="five by five" [6]="six")
declare -a mylist=([0]="bar" [1]="baz" [2]="three" [3]="four"
[4]="five by five" [5]="six")

Pop LAST element (dumped before and after):
declare -a mylist=([0]="bar" [1]="baz" [2]="three" [3]="four"
[4]="five by five" [5]="six")
declare -a mylist=([0]="bar" [1]="baz" [2]="three" [3]="four" [4]="five by five")

Delete element 2 using unset (dumped before and after):
declare -a mylist=([0]="bar" [1]="baz" [2]="three" [3]="four" [4]="five by five")
declare -a mylist=([0]="bar" [1]="baz" [3]="four" [4]="five by five")
```

Hashes

Also known as hashes, dictionaries, or dicts, associative arrays are lists where the index is an arbitrary string instead of an integer. They are amazingly handy for counting or "uniqueing" (that is, ignoring or removing duplicate) strings, among other things.

Unlike lists, these *must* be declared using declare -A, local -A, or readonly -A, and the subscript is always required; see Table 7-2 for an example.

Table 7-2. Sample bash hash

Element	Value
myhash[oof]	foo
myhash[rab]	bar
myhash[zab]	baz

The common operations on an associative array or hash or dict are:

- Declare a variable as an associative array (we say that instead of "hash" here because the flag is -A)
- Assign one or more values to it
- Display (dump) all values for debugging or reuse
- Reference one or all values (for, or for each)
- Reference a specific value (lookup)
- Delete one or more values
- Delete the entire hash

Again, rather than talk about all of that, we're just going to show you in Example 7-3, so pick out the idioms you need.

Example 7-3. bash hash example: code

```
#!/usr/bin/env bash
# hashes.sh: bash Hash example code
# Original Author & date: _bash Idioms_ 2022
# bash Idioms filename: examples/ch07/hashes.sh
#_____
# Does not work on Zsh 5.4.2!

# Books are not as wide as some screens!
FORMAT='fmt --width 70 --split-only'

# Declare a hash                                            ❶
declare -A myhash    # MUST do this, or `local -A` or `readonly -A`

# Assign to it, note no "+"                                 ❷
###myhash=(bar)         # Error: needs subscript when assigning associative array
myhash[a]='foo'         # Insertion 1, not 0...sort of
myhash[b]='bar'         # Insertion 2
myhash[c]='baz'         # Insertion 3
myhash[d]='three'       # 4 Different than our list example
myhash[e]='four'        # Insertion 5, note, not 4
myhash[f]='five by five'  # 6 Note spaces
myhash[g]='six'         # Insertion 7
```

```bash
# OR
#myhash=([a]=foo [b]=bar [c]=baz [d]="three" [e]="four" [f]="five by five" [g]="six")

# Display or dump the details and values                                    ❸
echo -e "\nThe key count is: ${#myhash[@]} or ${#myhash[*]}"

echo -e "\nThe length of the value of key [e] is: ${#myhash[e]}"

echo -e "\nDump or list:"
declare -p myhash | $FORMAT
echo -n         "\${myhash[@]}    = " ; printf "%q|"  ${myhash[@]}
echo -en      "\n\${myhash[*]}    = " ; printf "%q|"  ${myhash[*]}
echo -en "\n\"\${myhash[@]}\" = " ; printf "%q|" "${myhash[@]}"
echo -en "\n\"\${myhash[*]}\" = " ; printf "%q|" "${myhash[*]}"
echo -e "    # Broken!"  # Previous line is bad and no newline
# See `help printf` or chapter 6 "printf for reuse or debugging", we need
# this to show the correct words:
# %q    quote the argument in a way that can be reused as shell input

# "Join" the values                                                         ❹
function Join { local IFS="$1"; shift; echo "$*"; } # One character delimiter!
# Note the Join above requires "$*" and not "$@"!
echo -en "\nJoin ',' \${myhash[@]} = " ; Join ',' "${myhash[@]}"
function String_Join {
    local delimiter="$1"
    local first_element="$2"
    shift 2
    printf '%s' "$first_element" "${@/#/$delimiter}"
    # Print first element, then reuse the '%s' format to display the rest of
    # the elements (from the function args $@), but add a prefix of $delimiter
    # by "replacing" the leading empty pattern (/#) with $delimiter.
}
echo -n "String_Join '<>' \${myhash[@]} = " ; String_Join '<>' "${myhash[@]}"

# Iterate over the keys and values                                          ❺
echo -e "\nforeach \"\${!myhash[@]}\":"
for key in "${!myhash[@]}"; do
    echo -e "\tKey: $key; value: ${myhash[$key]}"
done

echo -e "\nBut don't do this: \${myhash[*]}"
for key in ${myhash[*]}; do
    echo -e "\tKey: $key; value: ${myhash[$key]}"
done

# Handle slices (subsets) of the hash                                       ❻
echo -e "\nStart from hash insertion element 5 and show a slice of 2 elements:"
printf "%q|" "${myhash[@]:5:2}"
echo '' # No newline in above
echo -e "\nStart from hash insertion element 0 (huh?) and show a slice of 3 elements:"
printf "%q|" "${myhash[@]:0:3}"
```

```
echo '' # No newline in above
echo -e "\nStart from hash insertion element 1 and show a slice of 3 elements:"
printf "%q|" "${myhash[@]:1:3}"
echo '' # No newline in above

#echo -e "\nShift FIRST key [0]:" = makes no sense in a hash!
#echo -e "\nPop LAST key:"        = makes no sense in a hash!

                                                                    ❼
# Delete keys
echo -e "\nDelete key c using unset (dumped before and after):"
declare -p myhash | $FORMAT
unset -v 'myhash[c]'
declare -p myhash | $FORMAT

                                                                    ❽
# Delete the entire hash
unset -v myhash
```

❶ Declare a hash (required).

❷ Assign to a hash.

❸ Display or dump the details and values; see Example 4-1.

❹ Two different join functions; see also "Comma-Separated Lists" on page 38.

❺ Iterate over the keys and values; see also "Comma-Separated Lists" on page 38.

❻ Handle slices (subsets) of the hash, which is rather odd, since the subscript is not an ordered integer list.

❼ Delete keys.

❽ Delete the entire hash. Beware of unset because there's a subtle catch. If you happen to have a file with the same name as a variable, globbing can hurt you, and you can clobber unexpected things. To avoid that, it's best to quote your variable. It's even safer to use -v to force unset to treat your argument as a shell variable, like unset -v 'list'.

That looks like Example 7-4 when you run it.

Example 7-4. bash hash example: output

```
The key count is: 7 or 7

The length of the value of key [e] is: 4

Dump or list:
declare -A myhash=([a]="foo" [b]="bar" [c]="baz" [d]="three"
```

```
[e]="four" [f]="five by five" [g]="six" )
${myhash[@]}    = foo|bar|baz|three|four|five|by|five|six|
${myhash[*]}    = foo|bar|baz|three|four|five|by|five|six|
"${myhash[@]}" = foo|bar|baz|three|four|five\ by\ five|six|
"${myhash[*]}" = foo\ bar\ baz\ three\ four\ five\ by\ five\ six|    # Broken!

Join ',' ${myhash[@]} = foo,bar,baz,three,four,five by five,six
String_Join '<>' ${myhash[@]} = foo<>bar<>baz<>three<>four<>five by five<>six
foreach "${!myhash[@]}":
        Key: a; value: foo
        Key: b; value: bar
        Key: c; value: baz
        Key: d; value: three
        Key: e; value: four
        Key: f; value: five by five
        Key: g; value: six

But don't do this: ${myhash[*]}
        Key: foo; value:
        Key: bar; value:
        Key: baz; value:
        Key: three; value:
        Key: four; value:
        Key: five; value:
        Key: by; value:
        Key: five; value:
        Key: six; value:

Start from hash insertion element 5 and show a slice of 2 elements:
four|five\ by\ five|

Start from hash insertion element 0 (huh?) and show a slice of 3 elements:
foo|bar|baz|

Start from hash insertion element 1 and show a slice of 3 elements:
foo|bar|baz|

Delete key c using unset (dumped before and after):
declare -A myhash=([a]="foo" [b]="bar" [c]="baz" [d]="three"
[e]="four" [f]="five by five" [g]="six" )
declare -A myhash=([a]="foo" [b]="bar" [d]="three" [e]="four"
[f]="five by five" [g]="six" )
```

A Simple Word Count Example

As we said, one of the most common uses of a hash is to count and/or "uniq" items,
so Example 7-5 is a simple but concrete example.

Example 7-5. bash word count example: code

```
#!/usr/bin/env bash
# word-count-example.sh: More examples for bash lists and hashes, and $RANDOM
# Original Author & date: _bash Idioms_ 2022
# bash Idioms filename: examples/ch07/word-count-example.sh
#_____
# Does not work on Zsh 5.4.2!
# See also: `man uniq`

WORD_FILE='/tmp/words.txt'
> $WORD_FILE                                                        ❶
trap "rm -f $WORD_FILE" ABRT EXIT HUP INT QUIT TERM

declare -A myhash                                                   ❷

echo "Creating & reading random word list in: $WORD_FILE"

# Create a list of words to use for the hash example
mylist=(foo bar baz one two three four)

# Loop, and randomly pick elements out of the list
range="${#mylist[@]}"                                               ❸
for ((i=0; i<35; i++)); do
    random_element="$(( $RANDOM % $range ))"                        ❹
    echo "${mylist[$random_element]}" >> $WORD_FILE                 ❺
done

# Read the word list into a hash
while read line; do                                                ❻
    (( myhash[$line]++ ))                                          ❼
done < $WORD_FILE                                                  ❽


echo -e "\nUnique words from: $WORD_FILE"                          ❾
for key in "${!myhash[@]}"; do
    echo "$key"
done | sort

echo -e "\nWord counts, ordered by word, from: $WORD_FILE"         ❿
for key in "${!myhash[@]}"; do
    printf "%s\t%d\n" $key ${myhash[$key]}
done | sort

echo -e "\nWord counts, ordered by count, from: $WORD_FILE"        ⓫
for key in "${!myhash[@]}"; do
    printf "%s\t%d\n" $key ${myhash[$key]}
done | sort -k2,2n
```

❶ We'll create a temporary file and set a trap ("It's a Trap!" on page 97) to clean it up.

❷ We have to declare `-A` the hash as a bash *associative array* (again, we say that instead of "hash" here because of the flag).

❸ Get the count of elements, or the *range* for the random number we want.

❹ Use the bash `$RANDOM` variable to pick a random list element (Example 4-3).

❺ Echo the random word into the temp file. We used three lines (callouts ❸, ❹, and ❺) to do something we could do in one line, like echo `"${mylist[$$RANDOM % ${#mylist[@]}]}" >> $WORD_FILE`, but we think that one line would be a lot harder to reread six months from now.

❻ Read the file we just created. Note the location of the file name *after* the done keyword in ❽.

❼ Increment the "key" value in hash for the word we saw in the line in the file.

❽ Note the location of the file name *after* the done keyword, from the loop in ❻.

❾ Iterate over the keys to display a list of the words, without duplicates, and without using the `uniq` external command. Note the `sort` command we did use after the done keyword.

❿ Iterate over the keys again, but this time display the "value" of the count as well.

⓫ Iterate over the keys one last time to display the count again, but this time sort the second field as a number (`sort -k2,2n`).

Example 7-6 contains the output.

Example 7-6. bash word count example: output

```
Creating & reading random word list in: /tmp/words.txt

Unique words from: /tmp/words.txt
bar
baz
foo
four
one
three
two

Word counts, ordered by word, from: /tmp/words.txt
bar     7
baz     6
```

```
foo     4
four    3
one     5
three   4
two     6

Word counts, ordered by count, from: /tmp/words.txt
four    3
foo     4
three   4
one     5
baz     6
two     6
bar     7
```

Style and Readability: Recap

In this chapter, we've demystified bash array (list and hash) handling and showed idiomatic solutions for the common use cases. While outside the scope of this book, there's much more to say about lists and hashes in bash. To learn more, see the following resources:

- *https://www.gnu.org/software/bash/manual/html_node/Arrays.html#Arrays*
- *http://wiki.bash-hackers.org/syntax/arrays*
- *http://tldp.org/LDP/Bash-Beginners-Guide/html/sect_10_02.html*
- *https://learning.oreilly.com/library/view/bash-cookbook-2nd/9781491975329*
- `man uniq`
- `man sort`

When you get the data structure correct, the rest of the code practically writes itself. When you get the data structure wrong, everything is a struggle. Bash has the building blocks for simple data structures, and once you get used to a little extra punctuation, they're not that hard to use and read. Just remember: you almost always want [@] and not [*], and refer back to our cheat sheet examples in this chapter when you need to.

Arguing

Some scripts are meant to do a single task; they need no variations. Many others, though, take arguments: one or more filenames, or options to provide variations on their behavior. Once you have more than a single option (or maybe two), you need to parse those arguments in an orderly fashion to be sure that you've covered all the possible ways that a user of that script might order those arguments. And come to think of it, even that single task script probably wants -h (or even --help). Let's take a look at how to parse those arguments and still have a readable, maintainable script.

Your First Argument

If your script just wants a single parameter, you can reference that in your script as $1. You might have statements like echo $1 or cat $1 as part of your script. We don't recommend using $1 throughout your script as it doesn't tell the reader anything about this parameter. It's better, for readability's sake, if you assign this parameter to a variable with an informative name. If the parameter is meant to be a filename, then choose a variable name like in_file or pathname or similar and assign it right away, early in the script. As we saw in "Default Values" on page 38, we can even supply a default value:

```
filename=${1:-favorite.txt}    # Or maybe use /dev/null as the default?
```

If the user doesn't supply any parameter when invoking your script, $1 will be unset. In the preceding example, the shell will assign favorite.txt as the value when parameter one is unset.

Need a second or third parameter or more? As you might have guessed, those would be $2, $3, and so on. They would be unset if no such parameter is supplied when invoking the script.

But what if you don't have good default values? Or what if you don't want to proceed when the user doesn't supply the correct number of arguments? Your script can check to make sure that the user has supplied the correct number of arguments by checking the $# variable. It holds the number of arguments supplied. If $# is 0, then the user invoked the script with no arguments. If $# is 1 but you wanted two arguments, then don't proceed. Issue an error message and exit (see "Exit Codes" on page 96):

```
if (($# != 2)); then
    echo "usage: $0 file1 file2"    # $0 is the script's name, as invoked
    exit
fi
```

We're only looking here at how to know that you've got the right number of arguments to your script. How you use all these arguments within the script is quite varied. We looked at some of those in Chapter 2.

Traditionally, when you wanted a list of all the arguments, you might have used $* to write something like `echo $*`, which works fine for this simple output. But once spaces were allowed as part of a filename, a slightly different syntax became the better choice.

Quotes are needed around a filename with embedded spaces in the name (e.g., "my file"), otherwise the shell sees that as two separate words. To refer to all the arguments to a script and have each one quoted, we use "$@" (string) or "${@}" (list). If we use "$*", that will give us one large quoted string containing all the arguments. For example, if we invoke a script like this:

```
myscript file1.dat "alt data" "local data" summary.txt
```

then "$*" would result in the single value "file1.dat alt data local data summary.txt," whereas "$@" would result in four separate words: `file1.dat` "alt data" "local data" summary.txt.

Yes, we know we talked about this in "Quotes and Spaces" on page 14 and then kept harping on it again in Chapter 7. It's just tricky and bears repeating.

Having Options

Options are ways to vary (slightly?) the behavior of a command. The classic (idiomatic?) way to specify options to a Unix or Linux command is with a single letter preceded by a -, called a *minus*, a *dash*, or a *tack*. For example, to have a command produce its long-form output, you might specify that with -l. Similarly, to have a command run in a more quiet mode (less output), you might specify -q right after the command name.

Not every command or script has these options, and not every command or script that has, for example, a -q option uses that option to specify a "quiet" output format.

It may mean "quick" in another command. It may not be a valid option at all in another command. These are conventions based on existing commands—tradition, so to speak.

It is worthwhile adhering to tradition, absent a compelling reason to abandon it. Among other reasons, it reduces the learning curve. What you learn about running some commands or scripts carries over into other commands. It also means that you can use the same technique for parsing options that others use.

Parsing Options

Use the `getopts` builtin command to parse the options to your shell script. It is called repeatedly (usually via a `while` loop) until all the options have been found. It assumes that all the options appear before any other arguments. It can recognize separate options (`-a` `-v`) as well as options that are bunched together (`-av`). You can specify that an option must provide an additional parameter. For example, you may want a `-o` option to specify an output file, so the user would invoke it with `-o filename` or `-ofilename`, both of which are supported by `getopts`.

Let's take a look at Example 8-1, which handles these kind of options.

Example 8-1. getopts argument parsing: simple

```
#!/usr/bin/env bash
# parseit.sh: Use getopts to parse these arguments
# Original Author & date: _bash Idioms_ 2022
# bash Idioms filename: examples/ch08/parseit.sh
#_____

while getopts ':ao:v' VAL ; do                                    ❶
    case $VAL in                                                  ❷
        a ) AMODE=1 ;;
        o ) OFILE="$OPTARG" ;;
        v ) VERBOSE=1 ;;
        : ) echo "error: no arg supplied to $OPTARG option" ;;    ❸
        * )                                                       ❹
            echo "error: unknown option $OPTARG"
            echo "   valid options are: aov"
        ;;
    esac
done
shift $((OPTIND -1))                                              ❺
```

❶ We wrote `while getopts` because we want to call `getopts` repeatedly, and the `getopts` command will return true when it finds an option (a dash followed by any letter, valid or not) and false when it reaches the end of the options. The `getopts` builtin needs to be given two words. The first is the list of options, and the second is the name of the variable into which it will put the option that it finds when parsing the command line. It will find only one option each time it is invoked, so we call it repeatedly via the while loop. In our example (':ao:v'), we want to support options a, o, and v. The leading colon tells getopts not to report error messages but rather to leave that to our script. The colon after the o character indicates that the o option has an argument that goes with it. VAL is the name of the variable that will be assigned if an option is found.

❷ Once getopts has been called, we can use the case statement to see which option was found. (See Chapter 3 for more about the case statement.)

❸ As for error handling, since we've asked getopts not to issue error messages, we need two cases to handle the errors. The first occurs if there is no argument supplied with the -o option. We have told getopts to expect an argument by putting the ":" after the o in ':ao:v'. If no argument is given when the script is invoked, then bash will set $VAL to be a colon, and it will set $OPTARG to be the character whose argument we couldn't find (in this situation, an o).

❹ Second, if the user supplies an option not in our list of valid options, then $VAL will be assigned the value of '?' (a question mark character), and it sets the shell variable $OPTARG to the option character it didn't recognize. We handle this with the wildcard pattern (*) in the case statement.

❺ There's one more important step to take when getopts is done and the while loop exits. The getopts builtin keeps track of its location in the command line arguments as it parses its way along, looking for options. $OPTIND is where it keeps the index of the next argument to be considered. Now that all those arguments have been parsed, we add a shift $OPTIND -1 to remove all the option-related arguments from further consideration.

Whether you invoke a script with myscript -a -o xout.txt -v file1 or just myscript file1, after the shift has done its work, $1 will thereafter refer to file1 because the intervening option arguments have been removed. The script's arguments are now just the remaining (nonoption) arguments.

Long Arguments

For some folks, a single letter isn't enough. They want full words or even phrases to describe the option they are invoking. The getopts builtin supports these, too.

We need to distinguish a long option from several single-letter options strung together (e.g., does -last mean -l -a -s -t, or is it a long option, the word last?).

The convention is that the long options begin with two dashes. (In this example, we would write `--last` to specify the long option.)

To use `getopts` to parse long options, we add a minus sign and colon to the option list, then add another `case` statement to recognize each of the long arguments. We include the colon *even if our long option takes no arguments.* (We'll explain that in the sections that follow.)

Example 8-2 shows the previous example, which parsed a set of options, expanded to include a couple of long arguments. The two long arguments that this will handle are `--amode`, which will be the same as the shorter `-a` option; and `--outfile`, which, like `-o`, takes an argument. For long options, the option and its corresponding argument can be provided one of two ways: as a single word using the equals sign or as two words. For example, when invoking the script, you can write either `outfile=file.txt` or `outfile file.txt` to specify the output file option. `getopts` and this second `case` statement can handle either format.

Example 8-2. getopts argument parsing: long

```
#!/usr/bin/env bash
# parselong.sh: Use getopts to parse these arguments, including long ones
# Original Author & date: _bash Idioms_ 2022
# bash Idioms filename: examples/ch08/parselong.sh
#_____
# Long arguments: --amode
#              and --outfile filename or --outfile=filename

VERBOSE=':'  # Default is off (no-op)

while getopts ':-:ao:v' VAL ; do                              ❶
    case $VAL in
        a ) AMODE=1 ;;
        o ) OFILE="$OPTARG" ;;
        v ) VERBOSE='echo'  ;;
#----------------------------------------------------------
        - ) # This section added to support long arguments   ❷
            case $OPTARG in
                amode    ) AMODE=1 ;;
                outfile=* ) OFILE="${OPTARG#*=}" ;;           ❸
                outfile  )                                    ❹
                            OFILE="${!OPTIND}"                ❺
                            let OPTIND++                      ❻
                ;;
                verbose  ) VERBOSE='echo' ;;
                * )
                    echo "unknown long argument: $OPTARG"
                    exit
                ;;
            esac
```

```
            ;;
#------------------------------------------------------------
        : ) echo "error: no argument supplied" ;;
        * )
            echo "error: unknown option $OPTARG"
            echo "    valid options are: aov"
        ;;
    esac
done
shift $((OPTIND -1))
```

How does this support long-format options? What's really going on here?

❶ Consider that getopts was designed to handle single-character options (e.g., -a).
   Adding the minus sign to the option list means that -- will be recognized as a
   valid option.

❷ Any remaining characters after the two minus signs are considered the "argument" to the -- option and are put in the $OPTARG variable. We can use our inner
   case statement to match the value of $OPTARG to the long option names that we
   want to implement.

❸ What happens, then, for the options, like --outfile, that need a user-supplied
   argument? If the argument is supplied with the equals sign syntax (e.g., --
   outfile=my.txt), then getopts assigns that entire string (after the --) to OPTARG.
   We can extract the argument from the option string using bash's parameter
   expansion string manipulation (see "Parameter Expansion" on page 32), removing (\#) all of the characters (*) up to, and including, the equals sign (=) via the
   expression that uses all of these symbols. That leaves us with just the characters
   after the equals sign, which would be the argument that we're after. We might also
   have coded it to be more literal with the string we want to remove by coding it as
   OFILE="${OPTARG#outfile=}" to remove that text from the front of OPTARG.

❹ When the argument is supplied as a separate word, the second outfile pattern
   in our case statement will be taken. Here we make use of a variable, $OPTIND,
   that getopts uses to keep track of its parsing. The filename argument is retrieved
   indirectly using ${!OPTIND}. How does that work?

❺ When using getopts, the shell variable $OPTIND holds the index of the next argu-
   ment to be processed by getopts. The ! says to use indirection—take the value
   of $OPTIND and use that as the name of the variable to retrieve. For example, if
   --output was the third argument encountered by getopts, then, at that point,
   $OPTIND would have the value 4, and, therefore, ${!OPTIND} would return the
   value of ${4}, which would be the next argument, the filename.

❻ Then we also need to "shift" $OPTIND since we've now handled it.

The rest of the script is as we've covered previously.

HELP!

There is a glaring omission in the preceding examples; do you need *help* to spot it? (That's a hint.) Right, -h and/or --help are missing. We strongly encourage emitting some kind of usage or help message on demand; it's discoverable and consistent with how most other tools work, and it's easy once you know how.

If you have a very simple script, Example 8-3 shows a quick-and-dirty solution.

Example 8-3. Quick-and-dirty help

```
PROGRAM=${0##*/}  # bash version of `basename`              ❶
if [ $# -lt 2 -o "$1" = '-h' -o "$1" = '--help' ]; then     ❷
    # Tab indents below, starting after the EoH (End-of-Help) line!
    cat <<-EoH                                               ❸
        This script does nothing but show help; a real script should be more exciting.
            usage: $0 <foo> <bar> (<baz>)

        As you can see, there are two required arguments, +foo+ and +bar+, and one
        optional argument, +baz+.
        e.g.
            usage: $PROGRAM foo bar
            usage: $PROGRAM foo bar baz

        You can put more detail here if you need to.
        EoH                                                  ❹
    # Tab indents above!
    exit 1                                                   ❺
fi
```

❶ We talked about this in "Shorthand for basename" on page 32.

❷ If the $# (argument count) is -lt (less than) 2, *or* the first argument is -h, *or* the first argument is --help, then use a *here-document* to display a help and usage message. (We discuss these in "Here-Documents and Here-Strings" on page 98.)

❸ Start a << (here-document) until we get to the EoH, which is end-of-help but could be EOF or anything else you prefer. It contains a -, so strip leading tabs (but *not* spaces) from the block, which allows you to indent in the code without indenting in the output.

❹ The end-of-help marker is also indented with a tab to match the rest of the contents.

❺ We can debate if exit code ("Exit Codes" on page 96) `exit 0` for success or `exit 1` (really anything greater than zero) for failure is correct there. If we asked for help, then we just got it, and it worked, so `exit 0`. But if we failed to provide the correct arguments, then we failed, so `exit 1`. Also, the script failed to actually do anything useful beyond showing a message, so that's arguably an `exit 1` fail. Pick a standard and go with it, but `exit 1` is a better fail-safe.

We've also inlined the help/usage message here, but it sometimes makes sense for that to be its own function so you can call it from other places if needed, as we'll see in Example 8-4.

Example 8-4. getopts argument parsing: long with help

```
#!/usr/bin/env bash
# parselonghelp.sh: Use getopts to parse these arguments, including long & help
# Original Author & date: _bash Idioms_ 2022
# bash Idioms filename: examples/ch08/parselonghelp.sh
#_____
# Long arguments: --amode and --help
#               and --outfile filename or --outfile=filename

PROGRAM=${0##*/}  # bash version of `basename`
VERSION="$PROGRAM v1.2.3"

VERBOSE=':'  # Default is off (no-op)
DEBUG=':'    # Default is off (no-op)

function Display_Help {
    # Tab indents below, starting after the EoN (End-of-Note) line!
    cat <<-EoN
        This script does nothing but show help; a real script should be
        more exciting.
            usage: $PROGRAM (options)

        Options:
            -a | --amode    = Enable "amode", default is off
            -d | --debug    = Include debug output, default is off
            -h | --help     = Show this help message and exit
            -o | --outfile  = Send output to file instead of STDOUT
            -v | --verbose  = Include verbose output, default is off
            -V | --version  = Show the version and exit

        You can put more detail here if you need to.
        EoN
    # Tab indents above!
    # If we have this next line, the script will always exit after calling
```

```
        # Display_Help.  You may or may not want that...you decide.
        # exit 1  # If you use this, remove the other exits after the call!
    } # end of function Display_Help

while getopts ':-:adho:vV' VAL ; do
    case $VAL in
        # If you keep options in lexical order, they are easier to find and
        # you reduce the chances of a collision
        a ) AMODE=1 ;;
        d ) DEBUG='echo' ;;
        h ) Display_Help ; exit 1 ;;         # We violated our style here
        o ) OFILE="$OPTARG" ;;
        v ) VERBOSE='echo'  ;;
        V ) echo "$VERSION" && exit 0 ;;     # We violated our style here too
#----------------------------------------------------------
        -) # This section added to support long arguments
            case $OPTARG in
                amode    ) AMODE=1 ;;
                debug    ) DEBUG='echo' ;;
                help     )
                    Display_Help
                    exit 1
                ;;
                outfile=* ) OFILE="${OPTARG#*=}" ;;
                outfile  )
                            OFILE="${!OPTIND}"
                            let OPTIND++
                ;;
                verbose  ) VERBOSE='echo' ;;
                version  )
                    echo "$VERSION"
                    exit 0
                ;;
                * )
                    echo "unknown long argument: $OPTARG"
                    exit
                ;;
            esac
        ;;
#----------------------------------------------------------
        : ) echo "error: no argument supplied" ;;
        * )
            echo "error: unknown option $OPTARG"
            echo "    valid options are: aov"
        ;;
    esac
done
shift $((OPTIND -1))

echo "Code for $0 goes here."

$VERBOSE 'Example verbose message...'
```

```
$DEBUG 'Example DEBUG message...'

echo "End of $PROGRAM run."
```

We've packed a lot into this example, but you've already seen most of it. We've built on the long arguments example to add help, but we also added a simple way to have *debug* and *verbose* flags and output. We now have a function for `Display_Help` because we need to call it from at least two places: short- and long-option handling. That should be pretty clear.

We also violated our `case..esac` style guideline for "one-liners" since the `exit` command makes it a multiline block. We could just as easily have expanded it (as we did in the long options section), but we've gone from one line to four lines for...no gain in clarity and a loss of three vertical lines on your screen that might better display more important code:

```
        h ) Display_Help ; exit 1 ;;
    # Versus
        h )
            Display_Help
            exit 1
        ;;
```

Debug and Verbose

In Example 8-4, we set a colon as the default value for the variable VERBOSE. That may seem an odd value, but consider the example use of that variable later in the script:

```
    $VERBOSE 'Example verbose message...'
```

In the default case (if the user does not specify verbose mode), then, to execute that line, $VERBOSE is replaced by a :, the no-op (no operation) or null command (which does nothing, ignores its arguments, and is always true). Thus no message would be printed. But if the user invokes the script with a -v or --verbose, then $VERBOSE is replaced with an echo, and the line to be executed would now, in effect, be this:

```
    echo 'Example verbose message...'
```

and the message will be printed for the user to see.

This idiom for conditional messages is simple code that's easy to write, easy to read, and even easy to grep for when writing documentation. You can use the same thing for DEBUG as needed.

Version

Just like `-h` and/or `--help`, a version command can be useful. First, though, is `-v` version or verbose? We prefer `-V` for version and `-v` for verbose (if applicable). Second, do you *need* a version? Not as much as you need help, so it really depends. The gen2 version-control systems like CVS and SVN made version easy—just use keyword expansion like `VERSION=$Id$`. But the gen3 systems like Git don't support that, so you're back to a manually updated variable, or some kind of build-time or CI (continuous integration) incrementer. For larger or public scripts, it makes sense; for smaller personal scripts, it might not. Your call.

You implement *version* by `VERSION=something` and display it the same way as *help*. Choosing the exit code ("Exit Codes" on page 96) of this is easier since you get the version output only if you asked for it, so `exit 0` clearly makes sense.

What you set `$VERSION` to is up to you:

- `VERSION=$Id$` for CVS or SVN
- `VERSION=v1.2.3`
- `VERSION="$PROGRAM v1.2.3"`
- `VERSION="$0 v1.2.3"` # Probably not, since $0 varies
- `VERSION=12`

Style and Readability: Recap

In this chapter, we discussed CLI options, arguments, and usage. We showed a simple way to parse a single argument and how not to proceed with insufficient arguments by checking `$#`. We then described the bash builtin `getopts` as a good way to parse both short- and long-format options.

A script that has any significant amount of argument parsing should make an effort to keep that code separate from the core function of the script. That is often best accomplished by setting flag variables in the case statement(s) that can be referenced later in the script where the functionality is implemented. You can make a big improvement in readability for your script by making the parsing of arguments a separate function in your script. Wrap Example 8-4 in a function definition:

```
# Called like: parseargs "${@}"
function parseargs {
    ...
}
```

then call it with `parseargs "${@}"`, and the remainder of your script can follow, using the flags set in the `parseargs` function.

Adding lots of conditional debug information or expanded (verbose) output can detract from terseness and overall readability when those statements are wrapped in if statements. They clutter and complicate the logic of the code. We showed an idiom that provides the same output choices but obviates the need for the if statements, making for a simpler coding style and easier readability.

Files and More

What makes a plain old file a shell script, and how do you emit exit codes? How do you read files? We'll talk about all that—and more—in this chapter.

Reading Files

There are three main idiomatic ways to read files into a bash script. Some of them "slurp" the entire file into memory, and others work one line at a time.

read

We've already used `read` for processing key/value pairs in Chapter 2, and we'll see it again in "Getting User Input" on page 104, but the other major use is reading files and parsing input one line at a time:

```
$ grep '^nobody' /etc/passwd | read -d':' user shadow uid gid gecos home shell

$ echo "$user | $shadow | $uid | $gid | $gecos | $home | $shell"
  |   |   |   |   |   |
```

Wait, what happened? Where's my data? Well, that's a gotcha—it went into the subshell created by the pipe (|), and it never came out. What about this?

```
$ grep '^nobody' /etc/passwd | { \
    read -d':' user shadow uid gid gecos home shell; \
    echo "$user | $shadow | $uid | $gid | $gecos | $home | $shell" \
  }
nobody |   |   |   |   |   |
```

That's slightly better, but where's the rest of it? Well, -d is the end-of-line delimiter, not the field separator ($IFS). One more try:

```
$ grep '^nobody' /etc/passwd | { \
    read -d':' user shadow uid gid gecos home shell; \
    echo "$user | $shadow | $uid | $gid | $gecos | $home | $shell" \
  }
nobody | x | 65534 | 65534 | nobody | /nonexistent | /usr/sbin/nologin
```

See also "Fiddling with $IFS for Fun and Profit, to Read Files" on page 89.

lastpipe

If you are running bash 4+, you can set shopt -s lastpipe, which will run the last command of a pipeline in the current shell so your script can see the environment. Note that this only works if *job control* is disabled, which is the default in scripts but not in interactive sessions. You can disable job control using set +m, but that disables CTRL-C, CTRL-Z, fg, and bg, so we don't recommend doing that.

mapfile

mapfile is also known as readarray, but they are the same command. Added in bash v4, mapfile reads a file into an array (list) and has options to read only -n count lines at a time, skip -s count lines, display a progress indicator (-c/-C), and more. This is much easier to use than other methods.

The simple use is, well, simple, and it "slurps" the entire file into memory, as shown in Example 9-1.

Example 9-1. Simple mapfile

```
mapfile -t nodes < /path/to/list/of/hosts  # -t removes newlines

# Loop around the nodes
for node in ${nodes[@]}; do
    ssh $node 'echo -e "$HOSTNAME:\t$(uptime)"'
done
```

Using -n is a bit more complicated, because while mapfile will continue to read nothing, so you have to check to see if it actually got data (${#nodes[@]} is nonzero) or you'll create an infinite loop (Example 9-2).

Example 9-2. Batch `mapfile` example

```
BATCH=10
# While we're reading data...    && there is still data there!
while mapfile -t -n $BATCH nodes && ((${#nodes[@]})); do
    for node in ${nodes[@]}; do
        ssh $node 'echo -e "$HOSTNAME:\t$(uptime)"'
    done
done < /path/to/list/of/hosts
```

Of course, you can get fancier, and add some runtime user feedback. You might also need to throttle your process for various reasons, so you can do something like the code in Example 9-3.

Example 9-3. Fancy `mapfile` example: code

```
#!/usr/bin/env bash
# fancy_mapfile.sh: Fancy `mapfile` example
# Original Author & date: _bash Idioms_ 2022
# bash Idioms filename: examples/ch09/fancy_mapfile.sh
#_____
# Does not work on Zsh 5.4.2!

HOSTS_FILE='/tmp/nodes.txt'

# Create test file                                               ❶
> $HOSTS_FILE
for n in node{0..9}; do echo "$n" >> $HOSTS_FILE; done

### ADJUSTABLE VARIABLES
#BATCH_SIZE=0  # Do the entire file at once (default); watch out for memory
BATCH_SIZE=4
SLEEP_SECS_PER_NODE=1     # Can set to 0
SLEEP_SECS_PER_BATCH=1    # Set to zero if `BATCH_SIZE=0`!

# Display runtime feedback to STDERR (so STDOUT can go into `tee` or a file)
node_count="$(cat $HOSTS_FILE | wc -l)"                          ❷
batch_count="$(( node_count / BATCH_SIZE ))"                     ❸
echo '' 1>&2
echo "Nodes to process:       $node_count" 1>&2
echo "Batch size and count:   $BATCH_SIZE / $batch_count" 1>&2   ❹
echo "Sleep seconds per node: $SLEEP_SECS_PER_NODE" 1>&2
echo "Sleep seconds per batch: $SLEEP_SECS_PER_BATCH" 1>&2
echo '' 1>&2

node_counter=0
batch_counter=0
# While we're reading data...    && there is still data in $HOSTS_FILE
while mapfile -t -n $BATCH_SIZE nodes && ((${#nodes[@]})); do
    for node in ${nodes[@]}; do                                  ❺
        echo "node $(( node_counter++ )): $node"
```

```
        sleep $SLEEP_SECS_PER_NODE
    done
    (( batch_counter++ ))
    # Don't get stuck here AFTER the last (partial) batch...
    [ "$node_counter" -lt "$node_count" ] && {
        # You can also use `mapfile -C Call_Back -c $BATCH_SIZE` for feedback but
        # it runs the callback up front too, so if you have a delay you'll
        # have to wait for that
        echo "Completed $node_counter of $node_count nodes;" \
            "batch $batch_counter of $batch_count;" \
            "sleeping for $SLEEP_SECS_PER_BATCH seconds..." 1>&2
        sleep $SLEEP_SECS_PER_BATCH
    }
done < $HOSTS_FILE
```

❶ Create a trivial test file for this example.

❷ This is not a "useless use of `cat`." Normally `wc -l` output is `<line count> <file name>`", but we want only the `<line count>`, and there is no option for that. When reading from `STDIN`, however, `wc` will not display a file name, which is what we want.

❸ Remember, bash does integer arithmetic only, so the batch count might have truncation errors.

❹ Integer arithmetic only; see previous callout.

❺ Did you notice we were lazy and did not put quotes around `${nodes[@]}` in the for loop? We can get away with that because we're reading hostnames, and they do not allow spaces. But it would be better to build a consistent habit and use quotes.

The output is shown in Example 9-4.

Example 9-4. Fancy `mapfile` example: output

```
Nodes to process:        10
Batch size and count:    4 / 2
Sleep seconds per node:  1
Sleep seconds per batch: 1

node 0: node0
node 1: node1
node 2: node2
node 3: node3
Completed 4 of 10 nodes; batch 1 of 2; sleeping for 1 seconds...
node 4: node4
node 5: node5
```

```
node 6: node6
node 7: node7
Completed 8 of 10 nodes; batch 2 of 2; sleeping for 1 seconds...
node 8: node8
node 9: node9
```

See also:

- `help mapfile`.

- Or `help readarray`, but that will just point you to `mapfile`.

- For a nice use of `mapfile` for cleaning up an AWS S3 bucket, see *https://oreil.ly/xie4t*.

Brute Force

Example 9-5 shows how the entire file is "slurped" into memory.

Example 9-5. Brute force file reading examples

```
for word in $(cat file); do
    echo "word: $word"
done

### Or, remove the "useless use of cat"
for word in $(< file); do
    echo "word: $word"
done
```

Fiddling with $IFS for Fun and Profit, to Read Files

`$IFS` is the "internal field separator," used in all *word splitting*. The default is *<space><tab><newline>*, or IFS=$' \t\n' using the $'' ANSI C (*https://oreil.ly/0Ol9N*) quoting mechanism, and this is fundamental to bash idioms. If you change `$IFS` without really understanding what you're doing, odd things may happen. In particular, the first character of `$IFS`, which is space by default, is also used in word expansion, and if you change that, chaos may ensue. If you really think you need to change the value of `$IFS`, either do it in a function using `local` or do it local to the command (see "Local Variables" on page 110). Example 9-6 illustrates this.

Example 9-6. Changing IFS for read example: code

```
#!/usr/bin/env bash
# fiddle-ifs.sh: Fiddling with $IFS for fun and profit, to read files
# Original Author & date: _bash Idioms_ 2022
# bash Idioms filename: examples/ch09/fiddle-ifs.sh
#_____
```

```
# Create test file (not spelling out "word" to keep output < 80 columns)
IFS_TEST_FILE='/tmp/ifs-test.txt'
cat <<'EoF' > $IFS_TEST_FILE
line1 wd1 wd2 wd3
line2 wd1 wd2 wd3
line3 wd1 wd2 wd3
EoF


#-------------------------------------------------------------------
echo 'Normal $IFS and `read` operation; split into words:'
printf '$IFS before: %q\n' "$IFS"
while read line w1 w2 w3; do
    printf 'IFS during: %q\tline = %q, w1 = %q, w2 = %q, w3 = %q\n' \
       "$IFS" "$line" "$w1" "$w2" "$w3"
done < $IFS_TEST_FILE
printf 'IFS after:  %q\n' "$IFS"


#-------------------------------------------------------------------
echo ''
echo 'Temporary $IFS change for `read` inline:'
echo 'Words are NOT split, yet $IFS appears unchanged, because only the read'
echo 'line has the changed $IFS.  We also shortened "line" to "ln" to make'
echo 'it fit a book page.'
printf 'IFS before: %q\n' "$IFS"
while IFS='' read line w1 w2 w3; do
    printf 'IFS during: %q\tln = %q, w1 = %q, w2 = %q, w3 = %q\n' \
       "$IFS" "$line" "$w1" "$w2" "$w3"
done < $IFS_TEST_FILE
printf 'IFS after:  %q\n' "$IFS"


#-------------------------------------------------------------------
function Read_A_File {
    local file="$1"
    local IFS=''

    while read line w1 w2 w3; do
    printf 'IFS during: %q\tline = %q, w1 = %q, w2 = %q, w3 = %q\n' \
      "$IFS" "$line" "$w1" "$w2" "$w3"
    done < $IFS_TEST_FILE
}

echo ''
echo 'Temporary $IFS change for `read` in a function; NOT split, $IFS changed:'
printf 'IFS before: %q\n' "$IFS"
Read_A_File
printf 'IFS after:  %q\n' "$IFS"
```

```
#-----------------------------------------------------------------
echo ''
echo 'But you may not need to change $IFS at all...  See `help read` and'
echo 'note the parts about:'
echo '    ...leftover words assigned to the last NAME'
echo '    ...[read line until] DELIM is read, rather than newline'
echo 'Normal $IFS and `read` operation using only 1 variable:'
printf 'IFS before: %q\n' "$IFS"
while read line; do
    printf 'IFS during: %q\tline = %q\n' "$IFS" "$line"
done < $IFS_TEST_FILE
printf 'IFS after:  %q\n' "$IFS"
```

The output is shown in Example 9-7.

Example 9-7. Changing IFS for read example: output

```
Normal $IFS and `read` operation; split into words:
$IFS before: $' \t\n'
IFS during: $' \t\n'    line = line1, w1 = wd1, w2 = wd2, w3 = wd3
IFS during: $' \t\n'    line = line2, w1 = wd1, w2 = wd2, w3 = wd3
IFS during: $' \t\n'    line = line3, w1 = wd1, w2 = wd2, w3 = wd3
IFS after:  $' \t\n'

Temporary $IFS change for `read` inline:
Words are NOT split, yet $IFS appears unchanged, because only the read
line has the changed $IFS.  We also shortened "line" to "ln" to make
it fit a book page.
IFS before: $' \t\n'
IFS during: $' \t\n'    ln = line1\ wd1\ wd2\ wd3, w1 = '', w2 = '', w3 = ''
IFS during: $' \t\n'    ln = line2\ wd1\ wd2\ wd3, w1 = '', w2 = '', w3 = ''
IFS during: $' \t\n'    ln = line3\ wd1\ wd2\ wd3, w1 = '', w2 = '', w3 = ''
IFS after:  $' \t\n'

Temporary $IFS change for `read` in a function; NOT split, $IFS changed:
IFS before: $' \t\n'
IFS during: ''  line = line1\ wd1\ wd2\ wd3, w1 = '', w2 = '', w3 = ''
IFS during: ''  line = line2\ wd1\ wd2\ wd3, w1 = '', w2 = '', w3 = ''
IFS during: ''  line = line3\ wd1\ wd2\ wd3, w1 = '', w2 = '', w3 = ''
IFS after:  $' \t\n'

But you may not need to change $IFS at all...  See `help read` and
note the parts about:
    ...leftover words assigned to the last NAME
    ...[read line until] DELIM is read, rather than newline
Normal $IFS and `read` operation using only 1 variable:
IFS before: $' \t\n'
IFS during: $' \t\n'    line = line1\ wd1\ wd2\ wd3
IFS during: $' \t\n'    line = line2\ wd1\ wd2\ wd3
IFS during: $' \t\n'    line = line3\ wd1\ wd2\ wd3
IFS after:  $' \t\n'
```

See also:

- "Local Variables" on page 110
- "Reading Files" on page 85
- "ANSI-C Quoting" (*https://oreil.ly/DFkqR*) on the bash man page

Pretend Files

We all know that UNIX, Linux, and (of course) bash expect everything to be a file, right? *Everything is a file. That is The Way.* But what happens if you need to process only part of the file? Perhaps you have a number of nodes that report statistics every time period, and you want to `diff` them to see if any nodes have appeared or dropped. Let's assume the files are tab delimited and have multiple records from each node with the node name as the first field, but you aggregate them over an hour, or day, or whatever.

You could use temp files, though that is pretty tedious:

```
cut -f1 /path/to/previous-report.log | sort -u > /tmp/previous-report.log
cut -f1 /path/to/current-report.log  | sort -u > /tmp/current-report.log
diff /tmp/previous-report.log /tmp/current-report.log
rm /tmp/previous-report.log /tmp/current-report.log
```

Instead you can use these "pretend files" to do the same thing:

```
diff <(cut -f1 /path/to/previous-report.log | sort -u) \
     <(cut -f1 /path/to/current-report.log  | sort -u)
```

OK, it's really called *process substitution* (illustrated in Example 9-8), but we thought *pretend files* sounded like more fun.

Example 9-8. Simple process substitution example

```
$ head *report.log
==> current-report.log <==
always-talking
always-talking
always-talking
always-talking

==> previous-report.log <==
always-talking
going-away
always-talking
going-away
always-talking
going-away
always-talking
going-away
```

```
$ diff -u <(cut -f1 previous-report.log | sort -u) \
        <(cut -f1 current-report.log | sort -u)
--- /dev/fd/63  2022-01-09 20:01:37.857658587 -0500
+++ /dev/fd/62  2022-01-09 20:01:37.857658587 -0500
@@ -1,2 +1 @@
 always-talking
-going-away
```

Drop-in Directories

An idiom that you see in a lot of different contexts is a directory into which you can
add or remove a file to achieve some effect. This is very handy for Linux distributions
that use package management systems like RPM (Red Hat Package Manager) or
Debian APT (Advanced Package Tool) because a package can add a file on install
or remove a file on uninstall without having to programmatically edit files. /etc/
cron.d/ is a perfect example; packages can easily add cron jobs when installed and
remove those jobs when uninstalled and not affect anything else.

We're big fans of this technique for configuration files, if supported. For example, you can have an /etc/syslog-ng/syslog-ng.conf file containing @include
"/etc/syslog-ng/syslog-ng.local.d", then you can drop files into /etc/syslog-
ng/syslog-ng.local.d/ to adjust the configuration as needed for a particular node.

It's very easy to do that in your bash code as well (Example 9-9).

Example 9-9. Include drop-in files

```
# Source local overrides IF any exist AND are executable
for config in /etc/myscript.cfg.d/*; do
    # Override files MUST be EXECUTABLE or they will be ignored, which makes
    # it easy to disable them.
    [ -x "$config" ] && source "$config"
    # Or change `-x` to `-r` to use readable instead of executable
done
```

This idea builds on the "Wrapper Scripts" on page 23, so you can build simple,
extensible, and yet powerful tools for yourself or your users. You write a simple
skeleton script with some logic to look an "action" command up in a directory, and
some glue code to pull those commands together and provide usage or help. You then
add a "template" for new modules or actions, and you or your users just copy the
template and fill in the details to easily add a new feature.

Using a Library

If you have a lot of code you use frequently, perhaps a Log function using printf %(datefmt)T (see "Getting or Using the Date and Time" on page 57), it can make sense to put it in a library to reduce "WET"[1] code and maintenance. Of course, as soon as you do, you run into the usual library issues: deployment and calling it. Deployment is up to you and your general process and practices, but we can help with calling it.

Ironically, you will have duplicate "boilerplate" code to call your library, and you can't extract that into a library or the import process becomes circular. But since you have a template for header comments and such (right?), you can just add the code shown in Example 9-10.

Example 9-10. Sourcing a bash library

```
# Source our library
source /path/to/global/bash-library.lib || {
    echo "FATAL: $0 can't source '/path/to/global/bash-library.lib'"
    exit 1
}
```

We could have defined GLOBAL_LIBRARY=*/path/to/global/bash-library.lib*, but for two uses in boilerplate code, it didn't seem worth it. If you're really clever, you'll build a global configuration of variables into that library, *and* you'll allow overrides for variables and maybe library functions using node-local drop-in directories (see "Drop-in Directories" on page 93).

Shebang!

What makes a plain old file a shell script? Shebang!

We think "shebang" sounds like a spell, and it is, in fact, a magical incantation to tell the kernel (not the daemons) what to do with your code. We're taking about that #!/bin/bash or possibly #!/bin/sh first line of your script, of course. #! cleverly acts as both a comment and a *magic number* to tell the kernel to look for an interpreter, in this case bash.

The most common bash shebang on Linux is #!/bin/bash, but you will often see #!/bin/sh and #!/bin/bash -, and you may see #!/usr/bin/env bash, #!/usr/bin/bash, or other paths.

---

1 WET: We Enjoy Typing, the opposite of DRY: Don't Repeat Yourself.

We recommend either #!/bin/bash - or #!/usr/bin/env bash. We strongly discourage #!/bin/sh unless you are deliberately restricting your code to Bourne shell compatibility, in other words not using "bashisms." You used to be able to get away with that on Linux, but many Linux distributions switched to using the *Debian Almquist shell* or dash for /bin/sh because it was much smaller and faster than bash for running scripts, like all the scripts used to boot the system. But it's a bad idea to use sh when you really mean bash because, as we just noted, it's fragile and obscures programmer intent.

#!/usr/bin/env bash is much more portable, because as long as bash is in the $PATH, it will go find it. That's great when bash is not in /bin/, which is the case on BSD, Solaris, and other non-Linux systems. The only problem is that the overhead of spawning env, then searching the $PATH, then replacing itself with bash is slower. With the resources in modern computers, that almost never matters, but if you are developing on a constrained system or running a *lot* of scripts or instances in a short time, that overhead adds up (Example 9-11).

Example 9-11. Shebang speed test

```
$ head examples/ch09/shebang*
==> examples/ch09/shebang-bash.sh <==
#!/bin/bash -
:

==> examples/ch09/shebang-env.sh <==
#!/usr/bin/env bash
:

$ time for ((i=0; i<1000; i++)); do examples/ch09/shebang-bash.sh; done
real    0m3.279s
user    0m1.273s
sys     0m0.915s

$ time for ((i=0; i<1000; i++)); do examples/ch09/shebang-env.sh; done
real    0m4.291s
user    0m1.313s
sys     0m1.425s
```

The other detail to mention is the trailing - we've shown. That's there to prevent a very old interpreter spoofing attack; see section 4.7 of the Unix FAQs (*http://bit.ly/ 2fdmYSl*) for details. The Linux kernel (but *not* other kernels!) treats everything after the first "word" (in this case /bin/bash) as a single argument, so we "use up" that argument with the "end of arguments" dash. Note that this is not needed in #!/usr/bin/env bash because the bash part itself *is* the argument.

Unofficial bash Strict Mode

Perl has a use strict pragma to "restrict unsafe constructs" that causes a syntax check or run time error if you do not declare and initialize variables before using them, among other things. The unofficial bash strict mode article (*https://oreil.ly/mZX7f*) makes the argument that the following does the same (in spirit) in bash:

```
set -euo pipefail
IFS=$'\n\t'
```

We don't quite agree on changing $IFS like that because that will break a lot of bash idioms (see "Fiddling with $IFS for Fun and Profit, to Read Files" on page 89). The author makes a good argument, but it might be a large effort to migrate legacy code for that. The set commands are great, though:

- -e will exit the entire script at the first error.
- -u will exit the entire script if you use an unset variable.
- -o pipefail will fail pipelines if *any* command, not just the last one, exits with nonzero.

Adding -u will break a lot of existing scripts, but the fixes will be pretty easy, and you may find some variable name typos you didn't know you had, which is the whole point. -eo pipefail will probably break less up front, and when that does "break" a script, it was probably already broken, but the error was masked and these options just unmasked the problem.

This is definitely worth considering and perhaps adding to your templates and style guide.

See also:

- *http://redsymbol.net/articles/unofficial-bash-strict-mode*
- help set
- *https://perldoc.perl.org/strict*

Exit Codes

Unless told otherwise, your bash script will exit with the exit (or return) code of the last command run. Sometimes that's fine, and other times you may need to exit earlier after failing a sanity check or for some other condition.

In bash, zero means *success* and nonzero means failure. This is the opposite of many other languages, but it's this way because there is only one way to succeed but many ways to fail, and you might need to represent which way you failed, like:

```
if grep --quiet "$HOSTNAME" /etc/hosts; then ...
```

The bash exit code is only eight bits, so the maximum value is 255, but you want your return code values to stay at or below 125 because 126 and above are taken, as shown in Table 9-1.

Table 9-1. bash exit/return codes

Exit/return code	Use/description
0	Success
1–125	User-defined failure
2	bash builtins incorrect usage
126	Command found but not executable
127	Command not found
128–255	Command exited with signal N-128

See also the GNU documentation about exit status (*https://oreil.ly/jkAnE*).

The command to exit the entire script with an "exit code" is, wait for it, exit n. The command to return from a function is, again, wait for it, return n, where "n" is an optional argument as defined previously. Remember that return returns an exit code, not values. The "n" can be any shell expression like 5 or $val or something more complex. Remember if "n" is not given, status is that of the last command run.

See also our discussion about exit 0 or exit 1 for help and usage in "HELP!" on page 79.

It's a Trap!

The trap builtin (help trap) allows you to execute code when the script receives a *signal*, which includes when it exits. That is a great place to have "cleanup" code that will work even if someone CTRL-Cs (but not if they kill -9) the script. You can also use it to run debugging code, but for this simple case, just use set -x or run under bash -x. Run trap -l to list all the signals your system supports or trap -p <signal> to show the trap commands associated with that signal.

The typical use of trap is to clean up after your script, as noted. The syntax is trap [-lp] [[arg] signal_spec ...], and while that arg can be self-contained code, it's probably cleaner to just define and then call a function instead. That looks something like Example 9-12 (output shown in Example 9-13).

Example 9-12. Trivial trap example: code

```
#!/usr/bin/env bash
# trivial_trap.sh: Trivial bash trap example
# Original Author & date: _bash Idioms_ 2022
# bash Idioms filename: examples/ch09/trivial_trap.sh
#_____
# Does not work on Zsh 5.4.2!

function Cleanup {
    echo "$FUNCNAME was triggered!  Cleaning up..."
}

echo "Starting script $0..."

echo 'Setting the trap...'
# Will call Cleanup on any of these 6 signals
trap Cleanup ABRT EXIT HUP INT QUIT TERM

echo 'About to exit...'
```

Example 9-13. Trivial trap example: output

```
Starting script examples/ch09/trivial_trap.sh...
Setting the trap...
About to exit...
Cleanup was triggered!  Cleaning up...
```

See also the GNU documentation about `trap` (*https://oreil.ly/KDuFJ*) and "bash Debugging" on page 120.

Here-Documents and Here-Strings

Other languages have similar constructs, like C's `/* ... */`, and Python's `''' ... '''`, but bash has some interesting idiomatic features for *here-documents* and *here-strings*. We used a here-document in Example 8-3, but there is more to talk about and decode.

Here-documents are used to contain and often display blocks of text without needing a lot of delimiters and commands.

Here-document syntax is `[fd]<<[-]["']word["']`, where "fd" is an optional (and rarely used) file descriptor, - is a flag that means "strip leading tabs but not spaces," and optional quotes mean "do not interpolate the contents." The word itself is *not* subject to parameter, variable, arithmetic, or filename expansion, or command substitution. Among other things, that means it can't be a variable. If any part of word is quoted, interpolation is not performed on the document. We recommend using only single quotes since they prevent interpolation elsewhere in bash so the meaning is consistent, unlike using double quotes.

In practice, using - means you can indent the here-document in your code (but only using tabs) while not having that indent present in the document itself later, and not quoting means you can use variables in it. As we saw in Example 8-3, that's great for displaying a usage message that includes the name and path of the script, without a lot of echo or printf lines and quotes. We also use it later for "Embedded Documentation" on page 115.

Here-strings look like [fd]<<<word, which seems similar, but in this case the word itself *is* subject to parameter, variable, and arithmetic expansion; command substitution; and quote removal. They are essentially a simpler here-document without a delimiter that results in a string, with a newline appended.

See the GNU documentation on here-documents (*https://oreil.ly/CsUWq*) and here-strings (*https://oreil.ly/ujM8B*).

Are We Interactive?

Sometimes your code needs to know whether or not it is running in an interactive session. It may need to know because it will change behavior, like asking for input, or perhaps you only want to set certain configuration options for interactive shells.

The GNU documentation on interactive shells (*https://oreil.ly/kbZE2*) says to use one of the following, so you will see these or variations a lot:

```
case "$-" in
    *i*) echo This shell is interactive ;;
    *)   echo This shell is not interactive ;;
esac
```

or:

```
if [ -z "$PS1" ]; then
    echo This shell is not interactive
else
    echo This shell is interactive
fi
```

You can also consider the -t FD test, which is true if the file descriptor is opened on a terminal. If you do not specify a file descriptor, 0 (STDIN) is used. You can combine that with another test, say for bash itself, such as:

```
# Only if bash in a terminal!
if [ -t 1 -a -n "$BASH_VERSION" ]; then
    echo 'bash in a terminal'
else
    echo 'NOT bash in a terminal'
fi
```

or:

```
# Only if *interactive* bash in a terminal!
if [ -t 1 -a -n "$PS1" -a -n "$BASH_VERSION" ]; then
    echo 'Interactive bash in a terminal'
else
    echo 'NOT interactive bash in a terminal'
fi
```

Note that we deliberately used [ ] (test) instead of the [[ ]] (bash conditional) because part of the point is that this code might run on something that is not bash and thus does not support [[ ]] (e.g., dash).

Summary

This chapter is about the idioms that sometimes aren't pretty that you need to know anyway. There are a lot of ways to work with files in bash, often involving redirection and/or pipelines, so we've shown some typical bashy patterns. Bash scripts are also files, so we talked about the magic incantation to make the file into an executable script or library, how to exit out and clean up, and other useful idioms. And while "here-documents" aren't exactly files, they often take the place of a separate file of text, or a files-within-a-file, and we've used them elsewhere, so here they are.

Beyond Idioms: Working with bash

Code tends to grow. Complexity tends to grow. Say it with us now, "There is nothing more permanent than a 'temporary' solution!" Etch that in stone and keep it in mind when you write code, when you think about writing code, and when you go, "Hey, I bet I could automate that."[1] Plan ahead. Be flexible. Keep it simple. And make it easy, for yourself and others.

OK, but…what?

This chapter is a collection of additional useful material we wanted to talk about that just didn't fit in anywhere else. We may arguably stray out of pure "idiom" territory here, but this is all about getting work done at a bash prompt every day.

When you write that "one-off," take a few extra minutes to use good names and add comments. At the end, take a few more minutes to think about how the environment and code might evolve and what changes or exceptions might be needed. It's a lot easier to add features and flexibility now, while all the details are clear in your head, versus six months from now. Is this code really "one size fits all" (ha!), or might there be exceptions? Can a `case` statement handle some tweaks based on $HOSTNAME or might you have to ask the user a question? Does your script need arguments, or temp files? Maybe it needs to make some $RANDOM choices? Keep reading.

Life these days is pretty busy, and work even more so. What can you do to make it simpler? Can you structure your source repository to match deployment targets, to make it easier to map what is going where? Can you write new commands (scripts) to remember options and details for you? Can you automate an otherwise tedious manual task? Probably. We hope we've given you a lot of tools to do all that in the

---

1 See the xkcd comic "Automation" (*https://xkcd.com/1319*).

previous chapters, but we have a few more ideas to enhance flexibility and quality of life to talk about before we're finished.

Prompts

There aren't really any idioms for the bash prompt. The prompt you get by default depends on where your bash came from and how the configuration files have been tweaked, and every user likes different prompt settings. But there are some things to be aware of.

We're not going to go into a lot of detail about how you control the prompt—that's covered in the bash documentation, the *bash Cookbook* (recipe 16.2 and elsewhere), and all over the web. See the following:

- *https://www.gnu.org/software/bash/manual/html_node/Controlling-the-Prompt.html*
- *http://www.bashcookbook.com/bashinfo/source/bash-4.2/examples/scripts.noah/prompt.bash*
- *https://www.tldp.org/HOWTO/Bash-Prompt-HOWTO/index.html*
- *https://sourceforge.net/projects/bashish*

We will briefly cover the different prompts, because there are some new and little-known features, as shown in Table 10-1.

Table 10-1. bash prompts

Prompt	Use	Default
PS0	bash v4.4+ pre-execution prompt	None
PS1	Bourne/bash primary prompt	`'\s-\v\$ '`
PS2	Bourne/bash secondary prompt	`'> '`
PS3	bash `select` prompt	`'#? '`
PS4	bash debug parameter	`'+ '`
PROMPT_COMMAND	command before $PS1	None

PS0

    This prompt is displayed by interactive shells after you hit enter on a command but before the command runs. It can be useful to display a "start time" or other marker just before a command runs (see Example 10-1).

Example 10-1. Example bash pre-execution prompt

```
PS0='Start: \D{%Y-%m-%d_%H:%M:%S_%Z}\n'

### Note the difference between the prompt time and the start time
[user@hostname:T2:L1:C5289:J0:2021-08-27_17:46:04_EDT]
/home/user/bash-idioms$ ls -1 ch*
Start: 2021-08-27_18:47:37_EDT
ch01.asciidoc
...
```

PS1

This is the main bash prompt, inherited from the Bourne shell, and it's where you spend almost all your interactive time with bash, so it's well worth understanding and tweaking. The prompt shown in Example 10-2 drives some people crazy, but it's useful because it gives you all the information you can possibly need, making it great to copy and paste into documentation or trouble tickets. There is one catch, though. The date/time are displayed when the prompt is displayed, and if that was hours or days ago, that can be confusing. You can hack around that problem by just being aware of it and hitting enter a time or two before you start a new command or session. Or, if you have bash v4.4+, you can use PS0, as in the previous example. Note that the C5275 command history number is great when you fat-finger a password into your bash history. Just history -d 5275 and you're all set. (See help history, and bonus points for omitting the history command itself with a leading space, per Example 10-13.)

Example 10-2. Example bash primary prompt

```
export PS1='\n[\u@\h:T\l:L$SHLVL:C\!:J\j:\D{%Y-%m-%d_%H:%M:%S_%Z}]\n$PWD\$ '

[user@hostname:T2:L1:C5275:J0:2021-08-27_16:51:20_EDT]
/home/user/bash-idioms$
```

PS2

This is the prompt you see when you hit enter but have not completed the command, possibly because you have not closed a quote or here-document.

PS3

The prompt used by the select builtin; see "select" on page 107.

PS4

This is the debug prompt, or maybe *prefix* is a better word, for when set -x is active. Note that the first character is duplicated as necessary to show the shell nesting level, so you want that to be clear. + is a good choice; see also "bash Debugging" on page 120. Example 10-3 is arguably busy, but it's informative.

Example 10-3. Example bash debug prompt

```
export PS4='+xtrace $BASH_SOURCE:$LINENO:$FUNCNAME: '
```

PROMPT_COMMAND

Example 10-4 shows a command to run just before $PS1 is evaluated and displayed. It's used for all kinds of things like updating the window title for GUI terminals; displaying dynamic details about your environment, like what Git branch you're in; or even doing some very primitive and insecure logging.

Example 10-4. Example bash PROMPT_COMMAND for logging

```
### This should be one line; it is broken to fit the page
export PROMPT_COMMAND='logger -p local1.notice -t "bashlog[$$];" \
  "SSH=$SSH_CONNECTION; USER=$USER; PATH=$PWD; COMMAND=$(fc -ln -1)"'
```

bash Time Zone

This isn't really a bash idiom, but it's a neat prompt hack. The bash prompt defaults to displaying the date and time in the system time zone, but you can export TZ=*UTC* or some other time zone to change that. That's useful if you prefer to keep your GUI in your local time zone but would rather have bash display UTC for documentation purposes, or to have local bash time displays match server displays. Note that the prompt TZ will not change until after you run an external command; just hitting enter or running a bash builtin will not cause it to update.

See also "Time for printf" on page 55 for more date and time handling.

Getting User Input

Most of the time, bash scripts get user input via command line arguments, but sometimes you might need to ask for input as well. The two common ways to do that are the read and select builtins.

See also:

- help read
- help select

read

read reads a line from STDIN or a file descriptor and assigns the words to a list of variables, or into an array (list) variable, and it has a number of really useful options (shown in Example 10-5).

Example 10-5. bash help for read

```
$ bash --version
GNU bash, version 4.4.20(1)-release (x86_64-pc-linux-gnu)
...

$ help read
read: read [-ers] [-a array] [-d delim] [-i text] [-n nchars] [-N nchars]
    [-p prompt] [-t timeout] [-u fd] [name ...]
    Read a line from the standard input and split it into fields.

    Reads a single line from the standard input, or from file descriptor FD
    if the -u option is supplied.  The line is split into fields as with word
    splitting, and the first word is assigned to the first NAME, the second
    word to the second NAME, and so on, with any leftover words assigned to
    the last NAME.  Only the characters found in $IFS are recognized as word
    delimiters.

    If no NAMEs are supplied, the line read is stored in the REPLY variable.

    Options:
      -a array   assign the words read to sequential indices of the array
              variable ARRAY, starting at zero
      -d delim   continue until the first character of DELIM is read, rather
              than newline
      -e     use Readline to obtain the line in an interactive shell
      -i text    use TEXT as the initial text for Readline
      -n nchars   return after reading NCHARS characters rather than waiting
              for a newline, but honor a delimiter if fewer than
              NCHARS characters are read before the delimiter
      -N nchars   return only after reading exactly NCHARS characters, unless
              EOF is encountered or read times out, ignoring any
              delimiter
      -p prompt   output the string PROMPT without a trailing newline before
              attempting to read
      -r     do not allow backslashes to escape any characters
      -s     do not echo input coming from a terminal
      -t timeout   time out and return failure if a complete line of
              input is not read within TIMEOUT seconds.  The value of the
              TMOUT variable is the default timeout.  TIMEOUT may be a
              fractional number.  If TIMEOUT is 0, read returns
              immediately, without trying to read any data, returning
              success only if input is available on the specified
              file descriptor.  The exit status is greater than 128
              if the timeout is exceeded
      -u fd     read from file descriptor FD instead of the standard input

    Exit Status:
    The return code is zero, unless end-of-file is encountered, read times out
    (in which case it's greater than 128), a variable assignment error occurs,
    or an invalid file descriptor is supplied as the argument to -u.
```

One really useful set of options is `-eip`, which allows you to prompt (`-p`) for data but provides a prefilled default value (`-i`) and allows using *Readline* features (like arrow keys; see Example 10-13) to edit the default before accepting it (see Example 10-6).

Example 10-6. Providing an editable default value for user input

```
$ read -ei 'default value' -p 'Enter something: '
Enter something: default value
### Then we use readline features, like arrow keys, to change it
Enter something: changed: default value

$ echo $REPLY
changed: default value
```

Another handy option is `-s` for asking for passwords without showing the password as you type it (Example 10-7).

Example 10-7. Prompting for a password

```
$ read -sp 'Enter the secret password: ' ; \
  echo -e "\n\nShhhh, the password is: ~$REPLY~"
Enter the secret password:

Shhhh, the password is: ~super secret~
```

For your quick-and-dirty script, you can also do something like this, but remember that there is nothing more permanent than a "temporary" solution:

```
    read -n1 -p 'CTRL-C to abort or any other key to continue...'
```

The timeout feature is also great for asking for optional input but not totally hanging the script if no one is there (see Example 10-8).

Example 10-8. Prompt for input with a timeout

```
$ time read -t 4 -p "Are you there?"
Are you there?
real    0m4.000s
user    0m0.000s
sys     0m0.000s
```

`read` is also used to read files and parse input, as we discussed in "read" on page 85.

pause

This one is mostly for fun, but if you remember the old DOS/Windows `pause` command, in bash you do:

```
$ read -n1 -p 'Press any key to continue...'
Press any key to continue...
```

select

As its name implies, select creates a simple menu and allows you to select a choice. It's up to you to remember to create exit or abort options, if you want them. A similar tool with much more power is dialog, but that's not a bash idiom, so we're not going to cover it.

A simple example:

```
#!/usr/bin/env bash
# select-ssh.sh: Create a menu from ~/.ssh/config to set ssh_target,
# then SSH to it
# Original Author & date: _bash Idioms_ 2022
# bash Idioms filename: examples/ch10/select-ssh.sh
#_____

#ssh_config="$HOME/.ssh/config"  # Real one
# Replace the trailing 'select-ssh.sh' with 'ssh_config'
ssh_config="${0%/*}/ssh_config"  # Idioms test file

PS3='SSH to> '
select ssh_target in Exit \
  $(egrep -i '^Host \w+' "$ssh_config" | cut -d' ' -f2-); do
    case $REPLY in
        1|q|x|quit|exit) exit 0
        ;;
        *) break
        ;;
    esac
done

# This is only an example, so echo what we would have done
echo ssh $ssh_target
```

At runtime, it looks like this:

```
$ examples/ch10/select-ssh.sh
1) Exit                  3) gitlab.com      5) mythtv-be01
2) git.atlas.oreilly.com 4) github.com      6) kitchen
SSH to> 1

$ examples/ch10/select-ssh.sh
1) Exit                  3) gitlab.com      5) mythtv-be01
2) git.atlas.oreilly.com 4) github.com      6) kitchen
SSH to> 6
ssh kitchen
```

Aliases

Since you are reading this book, you probably already know about the `alias` and `unalias` command, but we want to cover a few important points. First, best security practice is to use `\unalias` when you need to remove an alias. The leading `\` inhibits *alias expansion*, thus preventing a malicious `unalias` alias from causing havoc.

Second, some Linux distributions like to set "helpful" aliases for root or all users, so you'll want to explore the defaults in your distribution(s) and environment(s). In particular, you will see `alias rm=rm -i` and similar aliases for `cp` and `mv`, which you may or may not find desirable.

Examples 10-9 and 10-10 show two sets of aliases that you might consider using, perhaps in your `~/.bashrc` file. Put some or all of them in your `.bashrc` file in your home directory.

Example 10-9. Trivial DOS/Windows "compatibility"

```
alias cls='clear'            # DOS-ish for clear
alias copy='cp'              # DOS-ish for cp
alias del='rm'               # DOS-ish for rm
alias dir='ls'               # DOS-ish for ls
alias ipconfig='ifconfig'    # Windows-ish for ifconfig
alias md='mkdir'             # DOS-ish for mkdir
alias move='mv'              # DOS-ish for mv
alias rd='rmdir'             # DOS-ish for rmdir
alias ren='mv'               # DOS-ish for mv/rename
alias tracert='traceroute'   # DOS-ish for traceroute
```

Example 10-10. Example aliases

```
# Install `xclip` or `xsel` for Linux copy and paste
alias gc='xsel -b'           # "GetClip" get stuff from right "X" clipboard
alias pc='xsel -bi'          # "PutClip" put stuff to right "X" clipboard
# Or Mac: pbcopy/pbpaste
# Or Windows: gclip.exe/pclip.exe or getclip.exe/putclip.exe

# Cleaner `df`
alias df='df --print-type --exclude-type=tmpfs --exclude-type=devtmpfs'
alias diff='diff -u'         # Make unified diffs the default
alias locate='locate -i'     # Case-insensitive locate
alias ping='ping -c4'        # Only 4 pings by default
alias vzip='unzip -lvM'      # View contents of ZIP file
alias lst='ls -lrt | tail -5' # Show this dir's 5 most recently modified files

# Tweaked from
# https://oreil.ly/1SUg7
```

```
alias randomwords="shuf -n102 /usr/share/dict/words | perl -ne 'print qq(\u\$_);' \
  | column"
```

Sometimes it's useful to have the same command work differently on different hosts. You can easily do that with a **case** statement (Example 10-11).

Example 10-11. Different aliases for different hosts

```
case "$HOSTNAME" in
    host1* )  # Linux, but only has `xclip`
        alias gc='xclip -out'      # Send X selection to STDOUT
        alias pc='xclip -in'       # Send STDIN to X selection
    ;;

    host2* )  # Mac
        alias gc='pbpaste'         # Send Paste Buffer to STDOUT
        alias pc='pbcopy'          # Send STDIN to Paste Buffer
    ;;

    * )       # Linux default
        alias gc='xsel -b'         # Send X clipboard to STDOUT
        alias pc='xsel -bi'        # Send STDIN to X clipboard
    ;;
esac
```

Functions

One thing you can't do with aliases is pass arguments into the middle of the alias, but you can do that with functions, as we covered in Chapter 6. We're starting to get out of idioms and more into recipes here, but we can't resist the handy little function shown in Example 10-12.

Example 10-12. function mcd

```
function mcd {
    \mkdir -p "\$1"
    \cd "\$1"
}
```

Of course, that's very trivial, and doesn't do sanity or error checking, and doesn't allow for setting permissions (-m mode), but even this version is a great time-saver if you make a lot of directories. Note the leading \ inhibits *alias expansion* so we're sure to get the plain bash builtin. We'll leave expanding it as an exercise for the reader.

Local Variables

We talked about this in "Local Variables" on page 54, but to recap, the local command may only be used inside a function to declare a variable local to that function. That's a good programming practice, but if you need a "local" scope outside of a function, there is a way to do that, and a common variable to work with is the internal field separator $IFS. Normally you don't want to change $IFS, because if you do, all kinds of expected behaviors fail. But every once in a while, you do want to change it, usually only locally, and you can do that (even outside a function) by prefixing a variable assignment before a command, like this read command we'll talk about next:

```
IFS=':' read ...
```

See also "Fiddling with $IFS for Fun and Profit, to Read Files" on page 89.

Readline Hacks

Readline is the library bash uses to read and edit command lines. It may be used by other programs, but you can easily access it using read -e in your scripts. It has a lot of options you can change to tweak its behavior, and it seems many users are not aware of them.

You can explore creating a ~/.inputrc file (see the bind -f command), but just to play, you can add these to a ~/.bashrc file (Example 10-13).

Example 10-13. Readline tweaks

```
bind '"\e[A": history-search-backward'  # Like CTRL-R but right on the CLI  ❶
bind '"\e[B": history-search-forward'    # Same except forward              ❷
bind '"\C-i": menu-complete'             # Cycle through possible completions ❸
bind 'set completion-ignore-case on'     # Ignore case in completions        ❹

# These are bash, but feel related to "CLI behavior tweaks"
export HISTCONTROL='erasedups:ignoredups:ignorespace'+                        ❺
export HISTIGNORE='&:[ ]*' # bash >= 3, omit dups & lines starting w/ space+  ❻
```

❶ Binds the "up arrow" to history-search-backward, which means if you start typing a command, then hit "up arrow," it will search for that string in your history. You can do something similar with CTRL-R, but "up arrow" is faster and more intuitive. However, CTRL-R will find strings in the middle of the command, whereas this feature is limited to the beginning of the line.

❷ Binds the "down arrow" to history-search-forward, which is the same as item 1 except forward in your history.

❸ Instead of beeping and just sitting there when you hit TAB and the completion is ambiguous, start cycling through the options to complete.

❹ Ignore case in completions for filenames and commands.

❺ In saving your history, erasedups removes all previous lines matching your current line before saving history. ignoredups prevents saving previous duplicate lines, and ignorespace prevents commands that start with a leading space from being saved in your history. The end result of this is your history is much cleaner, because you don't have duplication, but you also lose any sense of the order and sequence of commands, since duplicate commands are removed or never saved. You can also omit commands from being saved in your history, say if they contain sensitive data, but note that they will still be visible in the process list!

❻ The same as previous, for backward compatibility with really old bash, just in case.

Using logger from bash

The logger tool (man logger) is great for sending logs right into syslog, but we would argue that it has a bug, in that the -t or --tag argument is not mandatory, and the default is just the username. We recommend what is shown in Example 10-14.

Example 10-14. logger tags

```
logger --tag "$0[$$]" <msg>        ❶
logger --tag "$PROGRAM[$$]" <msg>  ❷
logger --tag "${0##*/}[$$]" <msg>  ❸
```

❶ The simplest case is using $0 for the name of the script and $$ for its PID. The problem with $0 is that it will vary depending on how the script was called, and that's both noisy and inconsistent. We'd rather use the basename.

❷ If you are already using something like $PROGRAM to get the basename (Example 8-3), then use that with logger also.

❸ If you have not set something like $PROGRAM to the basename of your script, you can do it right in the logger tag. That's starting to get a little obscure, but it will work. Try echo "${0##*/}[$$]" to see, but it's a bit less interesting from the command line.

If you are doing your own logging, see printf and time in "Getting or Using the Date and Time" on page 57.

Handling JSON with jq

jq is not bash, but we want to cover this because JSON is very common, especially when working with cloud infrastructure, and we've seen some awful code out there using tools like awk, grep, and sed to try to handle parsing JSON. Use jq instead, if possible.

jq Is Not Always There

Unfortunately, despite how common JSON has become, jq is not always installed by default the way awk, grep, and sed are. It is not included with Git Bash for Windows either, which does include awk, sed, cut, grep, tr, etc.

Sometimes you can dodge the bullet. For example, for AWS you can use --output=text, then use the usual tools. Otherwise, you can install jq in your default builds or find hack-arounds using Python or other tools, which is outside the scope of this book.

The source code for this book includes an `atlas.json` file, so we can use that for some examples. If we'd like to find the title of this book, we can do that:

```
$ jq '.title' atlas.json
"bash Idioms"
$ jq -r '.title' atlas.json    # "Raw" mode, without the quotes
bash Idioms

### But `grep` also works...sort of
$ grep 'title' atlas.json
    "titlepage.html",
  "title": "bash Idioms",
```

What if we want to know if syntax highlighting is enabled in various output formats? That's trickier with grep but simple with jq:

```
### What do we have?
$ jq '.formats | keys' atlas.json
[
  "epub",
  "html",
  "mobi",
  "pdf"
]

### Bad; this has no context and is useless
$ grep 'syntaxhighlighting' atlas.json
        "syntaxhighlighting": true,
        "syntaxhighlighting": true,
        "syntaxhighlighting": true,
        "syntaxhighlighting": true,
```

```
### Good; this tells us that PDF output does have syntax highlighting
$ jq '.formats.pdf.syntaxhighlighting' atlas.json
true

### Better, but very confusing, show formats and syntax value, see jq docs
$ jq -r '.formats | keys[] as $k | "\($k), \(.[$k] \
  | .syntaxhighlighting)"' atlas.json
epub, true
html, true
mobi, true
pdf, true
```

Read JSON in Firefox

Firefox has an *awesome* built-in JSON viewer that can really help you get a handle on what you are looking at and how to get jq to cough it up. Simply save your JSON output as myfile.json, then open file:///path/to/myfile.json in Firefox.

Grepping the Process List

When you grep the process list, one of the processes in that list is your grep command, but that's not what you are looking for, so you'll see the idiom in Example 10-15 to remove the grep line.

Example 10-15. Don't do this

```
ps auwx | grep 'proggy' | grep -v 'grep'
```

We think that solution is just ugly and inefficient, and we like Example 10-16 better.

Example 10-16. Do this

```
ps auwx | grep '[p]roggy'
```

This works because the *string* "[p]roggy" in the process list does not match the regular expression /[p]roggy/ that really means "proggy". In other words, "[p]roggy" != "proggy".

Or, you can just use pgrep -fl, or worst case, the old pidof.

Rotating Old Files

Logging is good, and archives are good, but at some point you need to "rotate" or delete old files. There are many idiomatic ways to do that, so we'll talk about a few and make some suggestions.

Many approaches to rotating old files involve the excellent find utility, but a large number of those also use -exec and/or xargs, and with modern versions of GNU find, those are unnecessary. The old idioms are:

```
find /path/to/files -name 'some-pattern' -a -mtime 5 -exec rm -f \{\}\;      ❶
find /path/to/files -name 'some-pattern' -a -mtime 5 | xargs rm -f           ❷
find /path/to/files -name 'some-pattern' -a -mtime 5 -print0 | xargs -0 rm -f ❸
```

❶ This is extremely inefficient because it calls a new instance of rm for each file.

❷ This is more efficient because it will batch up files (xargs), but it will break and do unexpected things if filenames contain spaces.

❸ This can also handle spaces, but it's still more complicated than you need.

It's much simpler, if you are using GNU find and do not have portability concerns, to use the code in Example 10-17.

Example 10-17. Delete old files using find

```
find /path/to/files \( -type f -a -name 'some-pattern' -a -mtime 5 \) -delete
```

Here are some things to keep in mind:

- See man find and search for atime and mtime. -mtime +5 means the file was last modified *at least* five days ago, but the "five" is not exact; see the man page for a discussion of the details.

- For testing, use -ls or -print *instead of* -delete! But don't forget to change it when done.

- Be aware that find will recurse into any/all subdirs under the path, unless you limit that using -maxdepth.

- You want to use the ( ) for grouping (find just *these* things that match *all* criteria…then delete them), but you have to escape them to prevent the shell from interpreting them itself.

- An -a "and" operator is assumed between options in the expression; you can also use -o for "or" if needed. We like adding the -a anyway, because explicit is better than implicit.

- -type f means *type* of ordinary file, so it will ignore directories, links, etc.

- -name is obvious but case sensitive. You can use -iname for case insensitive if needed.

Embedded Documentation

Programmers have a reputation for not liking to write or update documentation. Sometimes that's true, and sometimes you have programmers like, well, us. But clearly, the more friction involved in writing or updating documentation, the less likely it is to happen. Your team's definition of friction and how to reduce it will vary, but one possible way to help is to embed the documentation in the code. Various languages have found different ways to do that, and you can do it in bash too.

You can always have comments, and we've shown some ways to use comments as part of usage or help documentation (see "HELP!" on page 79). And it's easy enough to have documentation *next* to your code, say myscript.sh and myscript.asciidoc. But you can embed real documentation, in wiki or markup language, inside the same file as your code, as shown in Example 10-18.

Note that this example is a mishmash of Perl POD (Plain Old Documentation) and generic markup; you should normally pick just one. POD is old and feels very clunky compared to Markdown, Textile, etc., but it has some nice conversion tools, especially for man pages, and may still be a good fit if you use Perl and/or those tools. For other markup, Pandoc is a great converter—for example, pandoc README.md > /tmp/README.html && firefox *file:///tmp/README.html*.

Be sure to read the example or output because we've, well, embedded some more discussion and tips. Also, the callouts will look off and out of order in the source code, because they only make sense in the final output. Just keep reading.

Example 10-18. bash embedded documentation example: code

```
#!/usr/bin/env bash
# embedded-docs.sh: Example of bash code with various kinds of embedded docs
# Original Author & date: _bash Idioms_ 2022
# bash Idioms filename: examples/ch10/embedded-docs.sh
#_____
# Does not work on Zsh 5.4.2!

[[ "$1" == '--emit-docs' ]] && {
    # Use the Perl "range" operator to print only the lines BETWEEN the bash
    # here-document "DOCS" markers, excluding when we talk about this code
    # below in the docs themselves.  See the output for more.
    perl -ne "s/^\t+//; print if m/DOCS'?\$/ .. m/^\s*'?DOCS'?\$/ \
      and not m/DOCS'?$/;" $0
    exit 0
```

```
}

echo 'Code, code, code... <2>'
echo 'Code, code, code...'
: << 'DOCS'
=== Docs for My Script ❼
```

Ignore the callout in this title; it only makes sense in the output later.

Docs can be Markdown, AsciiDoc, Textile, whatever. This block is generic markup.

We've wrapped them using the no-op ':' operator and a here-doc, but you
have to remember, it's not bash that's processing the here-docs, so using
<<-DOC for indenting will not work. Not quoting your marker will not allow
variable interpolation either, or rather, it will, but that won't affect your
documentation output. So always quote your here-doc marker so your docs do
not interfere with your script (e.g., via the backticks we'll use below).

All of your docs could be grouped near the top of the file, like this,
for discoverability. Or they could all be at the bottom, to stay grouped
but out of the way of the code. Or they could be interspersed to stay near
the relevant code. Do whatever makes sense to you and your team.

```
DOCS
echo 'More code, code, code... <3>'
echo 'More code, code, code...'
: << 'DOCS'
=head1 POD Example ❽
```

Ignore the callout in this title; it only makes sense in the output later.

This block is Perl POD (Plain Old Documentation).

If you use POD, you can then use `perldoc` and the various `pod2*` tools,
like `pod2html`, that handle that. But you can't indent if using POD, or
Perl won't see the markup, unless you preprocess the indent away before
feeding the POD tools.

And don't forget the `=cut` line!

```
=cut

DOCS
echo 'Still more code, code, code... <4>'
echo 'Still more code, code, code...'
: << 'DOCS'
        Emitting Documentation ❾
        --------------------
```

       Ignore the callout in this title; it only makes sense in the output later.

       This could be POD or markup, whatever.

This section uses a TAB indented here-doc, just because we can, but we
handle that in the Perl post processor, not via bash. :-/

You should add a "handler" to your argument processing/help options to emit
your docs. If you use POD, use those tools, but make sure they are installed!
If you use some other markup, you have to extract it yourself somehow.

We know this is a bash book, but this Perl one-liner using regular
expressions and the range operator is really handy:
```
    perl -ne "s/^\t+//; print if m/DOCS'?\$/ .. m/^\s*'?DOCS'?\$/ \
        and not m/DOCS'?\$/;" $0
```

That will start printing lines when it matches the regular expression
m/DOCS'?\$/, and stop printing when it matches m/^\s*'?DOCS'?\$/, except that
it won't print the actual line containing m/DOCS/ at all.

Add that to your argument processing as "emit documentation."

DOCS

echo 'End of code... <5>'

exit 0 # Unless we already exited >0 above

: << 'DOCS'
h2. More Docs AFTER the code **❿**

Ignore the callout in this title; it only makes sense in the output later.

This block is back to generic markup. We do *not* recommend mixing and
matching like we've done here! Pick a markup and some tools and stick to
them. If in doubt, GitHub has made Markdown _very_ popular.

Docs can just go *after* the end of the code. There's an argument for putting
all the docs together in one place at the top or bottom of the script. This
makes the bottom easy. On the other hand, there's an argument for keeping
the docs _close_ to the relevant code, especially for functions. So...your call.

But if this section only has an `exit 0` above it and is not wrapped in a
bogo-here-doc, this might cause some syntax highlighters to be unhappy, and our
Perl doc emitter will miss it, so you have to find a different way to
display the docs.
DOCS

And that looks like Example 10-19.

Example 10-19. bash embedded documentation example: output

```
### Running looks like this (`./embedded-docs.sh`): ❶
Code, code, code... ❷
```

```
Code, code, code...
More code, code, code... ❸
More code, code, code...
Still more code, code, code... ❹
Still more code, code, code...
End of code... ❺


### Emitting (un-rendered) docs looks like this (`./embedded-docs.sh --emit-docs`): ❻
=== Docs for My Script ❼

Ignore the callout in this title; it only makes sense in the output later.

Docs can be Markdown, AsciiDoc, Textile, whatever.  This block is generic markup.

We've wrapped them using the no-op ':' operator and a here-doc, but you
have to remember, it's not bash that's processing the here-docs, so using
<<-DOC for indenting will not work.  Not quoting your marker will not allow
variable interpolation either, or rather, it will, but that won't affect your
documentation output.  So always quote your here-doc marker so your docs do
not interfere with your script (e.g., via the backticks we'll use below).

All of your docs could be grouped near the top of the file, like this,
for discoverability.  Or they could all be at the bottom, to stay grouped
but out of the way of the code.  Or they could be interspersed to stay near
the relevant code.  Do whatever makes sense to you and your team.

=head1 POD Example ❽

Ignore the callout in this title; it only makes sense in the output later.

This block is Perl POD (Plain Old Documentation).

If you use POD, you can then use `perldoc` and the various `pod2*` tools,
like `pod2html`, that handle that.  But you can't indent if using POD, or
Perl won't see the markup, unless you preprocess the indent away before
feeding the POD tools.

And don't forget the `=cut` line!

=cut

Emitting Documentation ❾
---------------------

Ignore the callout in this title; it only makes sense in the output later.

This could be POD or markup, whatever.

This section uses a TAB indented here-doc, just because we can, but we
handle that in the Perl post processor, not via bash. :-/
```

You should add a "handler" to your argument processing/help options to emit your docs. If you use POD, use those tools, but make sure they are installed! If you use some other markup, you have to extract it yourself somehow.

We know this is a bash book, but this Perl one-liner using regular expressions and the range operator is really handy:

```
perl -ne "s/^\t+//; print if m/DOCS'?\$/ .. m/^\s*'?DOCS'?\$/ \
    and not m/DOCS'?\$/;" $0
```

That will start printing lines when it matches the regular expression m/DOCS'?$/, and stop printing when it matches m/^\s*'?DOCS'?\$/, except that it won't print the actual line containing m/DOCS/ at all.

Add that to your argument processing as "emit documentation."

h2. More Docs AFTER the code ❿

Ignore the callout in this title; it only makes sense in the output later.

This block is back to generic markup. We do *not* recommend mixing and matching like we've done here! Pick a markup and some tools and stick to them. If in doubt, GitHub has made Markdown _very_ popular.

Docs can just go *after* the end of the code. There's an argument for putting all the docs together in one place at the top or bottom of the script. This makes the bottom easy. On the other hand, there's an argument for keeping the docs _close_ to the relevant code, especially for functions. So...your call.

But if this section only has an `exit 0` above it and is not wrapped in a bogo-here-doc, this might cause some syntax highlighters to be unhappy, and our Perl doc emitter will miss it, so you have to find a different way to display the docs.

❶ When we run the script with embedded documentation normally, it's just the code that runs, as we expect and desire.

❷ This represents a block of code that would be run. Note that the embedded documentation following the block is ignored.

❸ Another block of code; embedded documentation preceding and following the block is ignored.

❹ Can you guess?

❺ This is the end of the code, preceding embedded documentation ignored as above, but we exit the script now, so docs below this point technically do not need a here-document, but it's still best to use one for consistency and to make syntax highlighters happy.

❻ Now we're emitting the documentation! In this case, we have an `--emit-docs` option, but you could use other tools to extract and process the docs.

❼ This is generic markup. It could be Markdown, Textile, whatever.

❽ This is Perl POD and is processed via the various `pod2*` tools.

❾ This block could be POD or generic; the point is that we indented it, so we need to handle that in our processing tool.

❿ As we discussed in ❺, this is after the end of the code.

See the following:

- *https://en.wikipedia.org/wiki/Pandoc*
- *https://en.wikipedia.org/wiki/Plain_Old_Documentation*
- *https://en.wikipedia.org/wiki/Markdown*
- *https://en.wikipedia.org/wiki/Textile_(markup_language)*
- *https://en.wikipedia.org/wiki/Asciidoc*
- *https://en.wikipedia.org/wiki/Comparison_of_document_markup_languages*
- *https://en.wikipedia.org/wiki/Lightweight_markup_language*

bash Debugging

We've talked about adding debugging statements to your code in "Debug and Verbose" on page 82, displaying values for debugging in "printf for Reuse or Debugging" on page 58 and in Example 10-3, but we haven't talked about interpreter-level debugging until now.

First, you can get a gross syntax check by running `bash -n /path/to/script`. Technically, `bash -n` means "read commands but do not execute them" (see `help set`), and it's similar to `perl -c`. This will not tell you about runtime errors, incorrect logic, incorrect options to external commands, and such. But it will tell you about unbalanced quotes, parentheses, and brackets; invalid syntax for bash builtins; and so on. This is a great command to run early and often when writing or changing your script.

There's a similar `bash -v` or `set -v` command that is "print shell input lines as they are read," but in practice that's not as useful as it sounds because it displays before shell interpolation, so you just get your source code spit back at you.

bash -x (*xtrace*), on the other hand, to "print commands and their arguments as they are executed," is very useful, and that's the next step in debugging. Run bash -x /path/to/script, and be prepared for a lot of output. See Example 10-3 for one way to make that output more useful. You can also turn *xtrace* on in the middle of your code with set -x and then later turn it off with set +x (yeah, that hurts our heads a little too, but once you turn it on using -, turning it off with + is at least memorable). Example 10-20 illustrates this.

Example 10-20. Simple debug example

```
### Without debugging
$ examples/ch10/select-ssh.sh
1) Exit                     3) gitlab.com       5) mythtv-be01
2) git.atlas.oreilly.com  4) github.com       6) kitchen
SSH to> 1

### With debugging (2 lone lines broken to fit)
$ bash -x examples/ch10/select-ssh.sh
+xtrace examples/ch10/select-ssh.sh:9:: ssh_config=examples/ch10/ssh_config
+xtrace examples/ch10/select-ssh.sh:11:: PS3='SSH to> '
+xtrace examples/ch10/select-ssh.sh:12:: select ssh_target in Exit $(egrep \
  -i '^Host \w+' "$ssh_config" | cut -d' ' -f2-)
++xtrace examples/ch10/select-ssh.sh:12:: egrep -i '^Host \w+' \
  examples/ch10/ssh_config
++xtrace examples/ch10/select-ssh.sh:12:: cut '-d ' -f2-
1) Exit                     3) gitlab.com       5) mythtv-be01
2) git.atlas.oreilly.com  4) github.com       6) kitchen
SSH to> 1
+xtrace examples/ch10/select-ssh.sh:13:: case $REPLY in
+xtrace examples/ch10/select-ssh.sh:14:: exit 0
```

You might want to take a look at "Unofficial bash Strict Mode" on page 96, which could unmask subtle problems when added later or prevent them when added at write time.

Dumping Your Environment

It is often helpful to log or dump your environment when running from cron, continuous integration, or other circumstances where the environment may change or differ from what you expect. You will see the external env or printenv used for this, but the bash internal set command will give you much more information, including functions. On the other hand, it's a lot noisier, so check them all out and decide which is best for you.

Environment Information Leaks

If you log or dump your environment, be aware that it will often contain sensitive information such as user names, passwords, API keys, and so on! You may want to modify your dump command to redact data, perhaps using sed or Perl one-liners:

```
set | perl -pe 's/^(SECRET=).*/\1<REDACTED>/g;'
```

As of bash v3.0, there is a --debugger flag and shopts *extdebug* option, but here we have to be honest and say we never use those options; set -x has always been enough. Running bash --debugger – /path/to/script is likely to result in:

```
/path/to/script: /usr/share/bashdb/bashdb-main.inc: No such file or directory
/path/to/script: warning: cannot start debugger; debugging mode disabled
```

If you see that, you'll need to check out the Bash Debugger Project (*http://bashdb.sour ceforge.net*), which is "a source-code debugger for bash that follows the gdb command syntax." That is bash version-dependent, so be sure to get the right one for your system.

See also:

- *http://bashdb.sourceforge.net*
- Example 10-3
- "bash Linter" on page 134
- "Debug and Verbose" on page 82
- "printf for Reuse or Debugging" on page 58
- "Unofficial bash Strict Mode" on page 96

bash Unit Testing

On GitHub (*https://github.com/kward/shunit2*), there is a "unit test framework for Bourne-based shell scripts, and it is designed to work in a similar manner to JUnit, PyUnit, etc."...that and "bash Linter" on page 134, which we'll talk about in Chapter 11, are pretty interesting.

Summary

Hopefully, these hints and tips will be useful in your day-to-day work with bash and in planning ahead to allow for future growth while staying as simple and flexible as possible. If you liked this chapter, you will also probably like the *bash Cookbook*, which has over 600 more pages of, well, useful recipes like this.

Developing Your Style Guide

The overarching theme of this book is writing idiomatic, yet readable, bash code in a consistent style, and we hope we've provided the tools you need to do that. Style is just another way to say "how *we* write things." Find some style guidelines, write 'em down, and stick to 'em. We've covered a number of important style considerations in this book, and there are some other guidelines we'd like to mention as well, things to keep in mind when designing systems and writing code. You can use this chapter as a starting point for your own style guide or just adopt it as is if you like it. The Appendix is the same material without the talking points, to use as a "cheat sheet," and you can get the Markdown or HTML code from this book's GitHub page (*https://github.com/vossenjp/bashidioms-examples/tree/master/appa*).

Keep the following high-level principles in mind:

- Above all: KISS—Keep It Simple, Stupid! Complexity is the enemy of security,[1] but it's also the enemy of readability and understanding. Sure, modern systems and circumstances are complex, so try hard not to make it any worse than it already is.

- The corollary, as Brian Kernighan famously said, is that debugging is twice as hard as writing the code in the first place, so if your code is as clever as you can make it, you are—by definition—not smart enough to debug it.

- Try not to reinvent the wheel. Whatever you are trying to do has probably been done before, and there's likely a tool or library for it. If that tool is already installed, just use it. No matter how hard you try, you are never going to be able to match the effort and testing that went into rsync, so just use it. If you find random code on the internet...well, think about that one for a bit.

---

[1] Really: "Complexity is the worst enemy of security" (see *https://oreil.ly/zMJLF*).

- Plan ahead for special cases or overrides, since they will happen. Take a page out of Linux distribution packaging systems and provide an `/etc/thing/global.cfg` for defaults that you can blindly overwrite, then allow for overrides in `/etc/thing/config.d/` or similar. See "Drop-in Directories" on page 93.

- If it's not in revision control, it doesn't exist! (And sooner or later, it will be lost and then *really* won't exist.)

- Document everything. (But you don't have to write a book about it…oh wait…) Write your code, your comments, and your docs for the new person who will join the team a year from now, when you've forgotten *why* you did it *that* way. Document what *didn't* work, and maybe why, and cross-reference things, especially things that you can predict can hurt you. (Yes, `rm -rf /$undefined_variable` turned out to be a *really bad* idea!)

- Keep your code and documentation DRY: Don't Repeat Yourself. As soon as you end up with more than one copy, it's guaranteed they will get out of sync sooner or later—the only question is when. Use functions and libraries; don't be WET (We Enjoy Typing).

"The Zen of Python" mostly applies to bash as well, and it's not a bad place to start. Try `python -c "import this"` or see the Python documentation (*https://oreil.ly/O2nYx*).

The bash Idioms Style Guide Is Not Portable

This *bash Idioms* style guide is specifically for bash, so it is not portable to POSIX, Bourne, Dash, or other shells. If you need to write for those shells, you will need to test and tweak this guide to account for the supported syntax and feature of those shells.

Be especially careful in Docker or other containers where `/bin/sh` is not bash and `/bin/bash` may not even exist! This applies to Internet of Things and other constrained environments such as industrial controllers. See "bash in Containers" on page ix and "Shebang!" on page 94.

Getting down into more detail, what types of things should be captured in your style guide? We'll cover some of them in the following sections.

Readability

Readability of your code is important! Or as Python says, *readability counts*. You only write it once, but you (and others) will probably read it many times. Spend the extra few seconds or minutes thinking about the poor clueless person trying to read the code next year...it's very likely to be you. There's a balance and a tension between abstraction (Don't Repeat Yourself) and readability:

- KISS (Keep It Simple, Stupid!).
- *Readability*: don't be "clever," be clear.
- Good names are critical!
- *Always use a header.*
- If at all possible, emit something useful for `-h`, `--help`, and incorrect arguments!
  — Prefer using a "here" document (with leading tabs) rather than a bunch of echo lines because there's less friction when you need to update and probably rewrap it later.
- Use `source` (instead of `.`, which is easy to miss seeing and harder to search for) to include config files, which should end in `.cfg` (or `.conf` or whatever your standard is).
- If at all possible, use ISO-8601 (*https://oreil.ly/6QyeH*) dates for everything.
- If at all possible, keep lists of things in alphabetical order; this prevents duplication and makes it easier to add or remove items. Examples include IP addresses (use GNU `sort -V`), hostnames, packages to install, `case` statements, and contents of variables or arrays/lists.
- If possible, use long arguments to commands for readability, e.g., use `diff --quiet` instead of `diff -q`, though watch out for portability to non-GNU/Linux systems.
  — If any options are short or obscure, add comments.
  — Strongly consider documenting why you chose or needed the options you chose, and even options you considered but didn't use for some reason.
  — Definitely document any options that might seem like a good idea but that actually can cause problems, especially if you commonly use them elsewhere.

For variable naming, watch out for generic variable names like:

```
`${GREP} ${pattern} ${file}`
```

That's very abstracted out, and maybe reusable, but it's also pretty context free. We've replaced the older `` ` `` with newer and more readable (we think), and definitely more nestable `$()`, but more importantly, the variables are less noisy because we omitted unnecessary `${}` and have meaningful names:

```
$($GREP "$re_process_errors" $critical_process_daily_log_file)
```

After a while, you'll see that you and your team find certain (dare we say it) idiomatic ways to express concepts and operations you often face. That's when it's time to write a style guide, if you don't already have one.

On the other hand, if you are submitting a patch or maintaining code, it's best to follow the conventions of that code unless you're going to restyle and possibly refactor the whole thing.

Comments

A lot has been written about comments: what, when, where, and so on. Following are style guidelines related to comments:

- *Always use a header.*
- Write your comments for the new person on the team a year from now.
- Comment your functions.
- Do not comment on what you did. Comment on why you did, or did not do, something.
   — Exception: comment on what you did when bash itself is obscure.
- Consider adding comments about external program options, especially if they are short or obscure.
- Use an initial capital on the first word of the comment, but omit ending punctuation unless the comment is more than one sentence.

Add *useful* comments that explain *why* you did something and your intent! For example:

```
continue # To the next file in for loop
```

In theory it should not be necessary to explain *what* something does if you write clear code. But sometimes bash itself is just convoluted or obscure, e.g., variable substitution (see "Path or Prefix Removal" on page 33), like:

```
PROGRAM=${0##*/}  # Basename in bash
```

Separators are often useful for delimited logical blocks of code. But don't add a closing separator at the bottom to "box" it out; that just adds clutter and reduces your on-screen lines of code by 1. Whatever you do, do *not* build boxes with characters on the righthand side! It's totally unnecessary, and you'll waste a lot of time getting it to "look right" up front. What's worse is that it's a strong disincentive to fixing or updating comments later, because then you have to go fix the box again.

Don't do this:

```
##################################################################
# Please don't build boxes like this!                           #
#                                                               #
# They make it VERY painful to edit the comments later, because #
# now you have to worry about the closing character on the      #
# righthand side.  This example isn't too bad, but it gets       #
# out of hand quickly.                                           #
##################################################################
```

Do this:

```
##################################################################
# Please DO build boxes like this!
#
# This one is easier to edit, because while you still have to
# worry about text wrapping, it's just a simple leading "#" when
# you do rewrap.
```

Names

Naming is *important*. We can't stress that enough. The difference between $file and $critical_process_daily_log_file doesn't seem like anything except some extra typing *now*, when all the details are in your head. But we guarantee if you take the extra time to really think about what you are naming and how it will read in the code, that will pay off soon, by reducing coding errors, and in the future when rereading, debugging, and enhancing. Following are style guidelines related to names:

- Good names are critical!
- Global variables and constants are in UPPER case.
  - Prefer not to make changes to global variables, but sometimes that's just much simpler (KISS).
  - Use readonly or declare -r for constants.
- Other variables are in lowercase.
- Functions are in Mixed_Case.
- Use "_", not CamelCase, in place of space (remember, "-" is not allowed in variable names).
- Use bash arrays carefully; they can be hard to read (see Chapter 7). for var in $regular_var often works as well.
- Replace $1, $2, .. $N with readable names ASAP.
  - That makes everything much more debuggable and readable, but it also makes it easy to have defaults and add or rearrange arguments.
- Distinguish between types of referents, like $input_file versus $input_dir.

- Use consistent "FIXME" and "TODO" labels, with names and ticket numbers if appropriate.

Consider how easy it would be to confuse these and use (or make an off-by-one typo) the wrong one:

```
file1='/path/to/input'
file2='/path/to/output'
```

This is much more intuitive to read and harder to type wrong:

```
input_file='/path/to/input'
output_file='/path/to/output'
```

Also, don't leave out two characters to save typing; just spell out $filename so you don't get it wrong later. Was it $filenm or $flname or $flnm or what?

Functions

Following are style guidelines related to functions:

- *Always use a header.*
- Good names are critical!
- Functions must be defined before they are used.
  - Group them at the top, and use two blank lines and a function separator between each function.
  - Do *not* intersperse code between functions!
- Use Camel_Case and "_" to make function names stand out from variable names.
- Use `function My_Func_Name {` instead of `My_Func_Name() {` because it's clearer and easier to `grep -P '^\s*function '`.
- Each function should have comments defining what it does, inputs (including GLOBALS), and outputs.
- When you have useful, standalone pieces of code, or any time you use the same (or substantially similar) block of code more than once, make them into functions. If they are very common, like logging or emailing, consider creating a "library," that is, a single common file you can source as needed.
  - Prefix "library" functions with "_", like `_Log` or some other prefix.
- Consider using "filler" words for readability in arguments if it makes sense, then define them as `local junk1="$2" # Unused filler`, e.g.:
  - `_Create_File_If_Needed   "/path/to/$file"   containing   important value`

- Do use the `local` builtin when setting variables in functions.
  - But be aware that successfully being "local," it will mask a failed return code, so declare and assign it on separate lines if using command substitution, like `local my_input` and then `my_input="$(some-command)"`.
- For any function longer than about 25 lines, close it with `} # End of function MyFuncName` to make it easier to track where you are in the code on your screen. For functions shorter than 25 lines, this is optional but encouraged unless it gets too cluttered.
- Don't use a `main` function; it's almost always just an unnecessary layer.
  - That said, using "main" makes sense to Python and C programmers, or if the code is also used as a library, and it may be required if you do a lot of unit testing.
- Consider using two blank lines and a main separator above the main section, especially when you have a lot of functions and definitions at the top.

Also, define a single logging function in your library (e.g., `_Log`), and use it! Otherwise you'll end up with a wild mix of logging functions, styles, and destinations. Ideally, as we said previously, log to syslog and let the OS worry about final destination(s), log rotation, etc.

Quoting

Quoting is pretty simple, until it's not, and then you get a headache. We know how this works, and we still end up doing trial-and-error sometimes, especially when trying to create a one-liner to run as another user via `sudo` or on another node via `ssh`. Add some `echo` lines, and be careful. Following are style guidelines related to quoting:

- Do put quotes around variables and strings because it makes them stand out a little and clarifies your intent.
  - Unless it gets too cluttered.
  - Or they need to be unquoted for expansion.
- Don't quote integers.
- Use single quotes unless interpolation is required.
- Don't use `${var}` unless needed; it's too cluttered.
  - But that *is* needed sometimes, like `${variable}_suffix` or `${being_lower_cased,,}`.
- Do quote command substitutions, like `var="$(command)"`.

- *Always* quote both sides of any test statement, like `[[ "$foo" == 'bar' ]]`.
  - — Unless one side is an integer.
  - — And unless you are using `~=`, in which case you can't quote the regular expression!
- Consider single-quoting variables inside `echo` statements, like `echo "cd to '$DIR' failed."` because it's visible when a variable is unexpectedly undefined or empty.
  - — Or `echo "cd to [$DIR] failed."` as you like.
  - — If using `set -u`, you will get an error if the variable is not defined—but not if it is defined but is just unexpectedly empty.
- Prefer single quotes around `printf` formats (see "POSIX Output" on page 56 and the rest of "Time for printf" on page 55).

Layout

Following are style guidelines related to layout:

- Line things up! Multiple spaces almost never matter in bash (except around =), and lining up similar commands makes it easier to read and to see both the similarities and differences.
- *Do not allow trailing white space!* This will later cause noise in the VCS (version control system) when removed.
- Indent using four spaces, but use TAB with here-documents as needed.
- Break long lines at around 78 columns, indent line continuations two spaces, and break just before | or > so those parts jump out as you scan down the code.
- The code to open a block goes on one line, like:
  - — `if expression; then`
  - — `for expression; do`
- List elements in `case..esac` are indented four spaces, and closing `;;` are at that same indent level. Blocks for each item are also indented four spaces.
  - — One-line elements should be closed with `;;` on the same line.
  - — Prefer lining up the `)` in each element, unless it gets cluttered or out of hand.
  - — See the example code in Example 8-4.

There's an argument about not bothering to break lines at 70–80 columns that assumes everyone is using a wide graphical terminal and an IDE. First, depending on the team and person, that may not be true, and second, even if it is, when it *really* breaks and you end up debugging under fire in vi on an 80 × 24 console, you will not appreciate 200+ column code.

Break your lines.

Break them just *before* the important part, so when you scan down the left side of the column, the continuations jump out. We also like to use half the usual indent for broken lines. We can't do a good (bad?) long line here in this book because it will just break in odd places anyway. But we can provide a simple, and we think readable, example:

```
    ... Lots of code, indented a ways...
        /long/path/to/some/interesting/command \
        | grep    "$re_stuff_we_care_about" \
        | grep -v "$re_stuff_to_ignore" \
        | /path/to/email_or_log_command ...
    ...more code
```

Syntax

Following are style guidelines related to syntax:

- Use #!/bin/bash - or #!/usr/bin/env bash when writing bash code, not #!/bin/sh.
- Use $@ unless you are *really* sure you need $*.
- Use == instead of = for equality, to reduce confusion with assignment.
- Use $() instead of `` backticks/backquotes.
- Use [[instead of [(unless you need [for portability, e.g., dash).
- Use (( )) and $(( )) as needed for integer arithmetic; avoid let and expr.
- Use [[expression]] && block or [[expression]] || block when it is simple and readable to do so. Do not use [[expression]] && block || block because that doesn't do what you think it does; use if .. then .. (elif ..) else .. fi for that.
- Consider using "Unofficial bash Strict Mode" (see "Unofficial bash Strict Mode" on page 96).
  - set -euo pipefail will prevent or unmask many simple errors.
  - Watch out for this one, and use it carefully (if you use it at all): IFS=$'\n\t'.

Other

Other guidelines:

- For "system" scripts, log to syslog and let the OS worry about final destination(s), log rotation, etc.
- Error messages should go to STDERR, like `echo 'A Bad Thing happened' 1>&2`.
- Sanity-check that external tools are available using `[ -x /path/to/tool ] || { …error code block… }`.
- Provide useful messages when things fail.
- Set `exit` codes, especially when you fail.

Script Template

This is a sample skeleton or template script you can copy as a reminder and to save some (OK, maybe quite a lot of) typing when you create a new script:

```
#!/bin/bash -
# Or possibly: #!/usr/bin/env bash
# <Name>: <description>
# Original Author & date:
# Current maintainer?
# Copyright/License?
# Where this code belongs?  (Hosts, paths, etc.)
# Project/repo?
# Caveats/gotchas?
# Usage?  (Better to have `-h` and/or `--help` options!)
# $URL$  # If using SVN
ID=''    # If using SVN
#_____
PROGRAM=${0##*/}  # bash version of `basename`

# Unofficial bash Strict Mode?
#set -euo pipefail
### CAREFUL: IFS=$'\n\t'

# GLOBAL and constant variables are in UPPER case
LOG_DIR='/path/to/log/dir'

### Consider adding argument handling to YOUR template; see:
# examples/ch08/parseit.sh
# examples/ch08/parselong.sh
# examples/ch08/parselonghelp.sh

# Functions are in Mixed Case
##############################################################
```

```
    # Define functions

    #- - - - - - - - - - - - - - - - - - - - - - - - - - - - - - - - - - - - - - - - - - - - - - - - - - - - - - - -
    # Example function
    # Globals: none
    # Input:    nothing
    # Output:   nothing
    function Foo {
        local var1="$1"
        ...
    } # End of function foo


    #- - - - - - - - - - - - - - - - - - - - - - - - - - - - - - - - - - - - - - - - - - - - - - - - - - - - - - -
    # Another example function
    # Globals: none
    # Input:    nothing
    # Output:   nothing
    function Bar {
        local var1="$1"
        ...
    } # End of function bar


    #####################################################################################
    # Main

    # Code...
```

Other Style Guides

We strongly suggest you have a style guide and use it! If you don't like ours, and you don't want to tweak it yourself, you can go steal one from someplace else:

- The Google Shell Style Guide (*https://oreil.ly/HWaSV*)

  While we have a few quibbles and disagreements with this, it's very good and quite extensive. At best, you can just use it, and at worst, it's a place to start. There is a lot to like, and you could do worse (like not having anything), and a lot of other projects have adopted it, so…

  Among other things, we don't agree with:

  — The hundred-line limit. We see the point, especially for an environment like Google's, but we've got lots of scripts over that limit that are "mostly calling other utilities and are doing relatively little data manipulation."

  — "Indent two spaces" is a bit shallow for us; we like two spaces for continued lines and four spaces otherwise.

  — "${var}" is too busy. We prefer "$var" when possible.

— `function cleanup() {?` Ouch, no.

— `;;` closes the `case..esac` block and belongs at the same indent as the block opener, not at the indent of the code in the block.

- The following are other guides you can look at:

    — *https://linuxcommand.org/lc3_adv_standards.php*

    — *https://www.ovirt.org/develop/infra/infra-bash-style-guide.html*

    — *https://wiki.bash-hackers.org/scripting/style*

    — *http://mywiki.wooledge.org/BashGuide/Practices*

        — Great info: *http://mywiki.wooledge.org/BashPitfalls*

- Or do a web search for:

    — `"Shell Style Guide"`

    — `"Bash Style Guide"`

    — `"Shell script coding standards"`

bash Linter

Using a *linter* instead of or in addition to a style guide can also be handy. To be honest, we don't use one, but we thought we should cover it. The one we know about is `shellcheck`, and we have mixed feelings about the results; it's especially picky about quoting, and we don't always agree with its suggestions on quoting or in general, but those things are somewhat adjustable. That said, it's still very cool, and worth checking out.

- bash linter: *https://www.shellcheck.net*

    — *https://github.com/koalaman/shellcheck* (Haskell)

    — History: *https://www.vidarholen.net/contents/blog/?p=859*

    — Checks: *https://github.com/koalaman/shellcheck/wiki/Checks*

    — Tweaking: *https://github.com/koalaman/shellcheck/wiki/Directive*

    — Ignoring errors: *https://github.com/koalaman/shellcheck/wiki/Ignore*

    — Note, Eol (2020) CentOS-6 is too old: *https://github.com/koalaman/shellcheck/wiki/CentOS6*

If you install through your package system, remember that the version may be quite old. The Linux version is a tarball containing a single compiled binary, though, so it's easy to drop a current version in your path somewhere.

Summary

Hopefully, this book has given you a better understanding of how to read and write "bashy" code, and this chapter has provided a place to get started on defining a style (and guide) that will work for you.

Happy bashing!

The bash Idioms Style Guide

This is a copy of the points in Chapter 11 but without the commentary and examples. There's also a Markdown file in the examples directory so you can download and tweak it as desired, then render or include it as needed using pandoc or some other tool. Get the code from the book's GitHub page (*https://github.com/vos senjp/bashidioms-examples/tree/master/appa*).

The bash Idioms Style Guide Is Not Portable

This *bash Idioms* style guide is specifically for bash, so it is not portable to POSIX, Bourne, Dash, or other shells. If you need to write for those shells, you will need to test and tweak this guide to account for the supported syntax and feature of those shells.

Be especially careful in Docker or other containers where /bin/sh is not bash and /bin/bash may not even exist! This applies to Internet of Things and other constrained environments such as industrial controllers. See "bash in Containers" on page ix and "Shebang!" on page 94.

Readability

Readability of your code is important! Or as Python says, *readability counts*. You only write it once, but you (and others) will probably read it many times. Spend the extra few seconds or minutes thinking about the poor clueless person trying to read the code next year...it's very likely to be you. There's a balance and a tension between abstraction (Don't Repeat Yourself) and readability:

- KISS (Keep It Simple, Stupid!).
- *Readability*: don't be "clever," be clear.

- Good names are critical!
- *Always use a header.*
- If at all possible, emit something useful for `-h`, `--help`, and incorrect arguments!
  - Prefer using a "here" document (with leading tabs) rather than a bunch of echo lines because there's less friction when you need to update and probably rewrap it later.
- Use `source` (instead of `.`, which is easy to miss seeing and harder to search for) to include config files, which should end in `.cfg` (or `.conf` or whatever your standard is).
- If at all possible, use ISO-8601 (*https://oreil.ly/6QyeH*) dates for everything.
- If at all possible, keep lists of things in alphabetical order; this prevents duplication and makes it easier to add or remove items. Examples include IP addresses (use GNU `sort -V`), hostnames, packages to install, `case` statements, and contents of variables or arrays/lists.
- If possible, use long arguments to commands for readability, e.g., use `diff --quiet` instead of `diff -q`, though watch out for portability to non-GNU/Linux systems.
  - If any options are short or obscure, add comments.
  - Strongly consider documenting why you chose or needed the options you chose, and even options you considered but didn't use for some reason.
  - Definitely document any options that might seem like a good idea but that actually can cause problems, especially if you commonly use them elsewhere.

Comments

- *Always use a header.*
- Write your comments for the new person on the team a year from now.
- Comment your functions.
- Do not comment on what you did. Comment on why you did, or did not do, something.
  - Exception: comment on what you did when bash itself is obscure.
- Consider adding comments about external program options, especially if they are short or obscure.
- Use an initial capital on the first word of the comment, but omit ending punctuation unless the comment is more than one sentence.

Names

- Good names are critical!
- Global variables and constants are in UPPER case.
  - Prefer not to make changes to global variables, but sometimes that's just much simpler (KISS).
  - Use `readonly` or `declare -r` for constants.
- Other variables are in lowercase.
- Functions are in Mixed_Case.
- Use "_", not CamelCase, in place of space (remember, "-" is not allowed in variable names).
- Use bash arrays carefully; they can be hard to read (see Chapter 7). `for var in $regular_var` often works as well.
- Replace $1, $2, .. $N with readable names ASAP.
  - That makes everything much more debuggable and readable, but it also makes it easy to have defaults and add or rearrange arguments.
- Distinguish between types of referents, like `$input_file` versus `$input_dir`.
- Use consistent "FIXME" and "TODO" labels, with names and ticket numbers if appropriate.

Functions

- *Always use a header.*
- Good names are critical!
- Functions must be defined before they are used.
  - Group them at the top, and use two blank lines and a function separator between each function.
  - Do *not* intersperse code between functions!
- Use Camel_Case and "_" to make function names stand out from variable names.
- Use `function My_Func_Name {` instead of `My_Func_Name() {` because it's clearer and easier to `grep -P '^\s*function '`.
- Each function should have comments defining what it does, inputs (including GLOBALS), and outputs.
- When you have useful, standalone pieces of code, or any time you use the same (or substantially similar) block of code more than once, make them into

functions. If they are very common, like logging or emailing, consider creating a "library," that is, a single common file you can source as needed.

— Prefix "library" functions with "_", like _Log or some other prefix.

- Consider using "filler" words for readability in arguments if it makes sense, then define them as local junk1="$2" # Unused filler, e.g.:

  — _Create_File_If_Needed "/path/to/$file" containing *important value*

- Do use the local builtin when setting variables in functions.

  — But be aware that successfully being "local," it will mask a failed return code, so declare and assign it on separate lines if using command substitution, like local my_input and then my_input="$(some-command)".

- For any function longer than about 25 lines, close it with } # End of function MyFuncName to make it easier to track where you are in the code on your screen. For functions shorter than 25 lines, this is optional but encouraged unless it gets too cluttered.

- Don't use a main function; it's almost always just an unnecessary layer.

  — That said, using "main" makes sense to Python and C programmers, or if the code is also used as a library, and it may be required if you do a lot of unit testing.

- Consider using two blank lines and a main separator above the main section, especially when you have a lot of functions and definitions at the top.

Quoting

- Do put quotes around variables and strings because it makes them stand out a little and clarifies your intent.

  — Unless it gets too cluttered.

  — Or they need to be unquoted for expansion.

- Don't quote integers.

- Use single quotes unless interpolation is required.

- Don't use ${var} unless needed; it's too cluttered.

  — But that *is* needed sometimes, like ${variable}_suffix or ${being_lower_cased,,}.

- Do quote command substitutions, like var="$(command)".

- *Always* quote both sides of any test statement, like [["$foo" == 'bar']].

  — Unless one side is an integer.

— And unless you are using ~=, in which case you can't quote the regular expression!

- Consider single-quoting variables inside `echo` statements, like `echo "cd to '$DIR' failed."` because it's visible when a variable is unexpectedly undefined or empty.

  — Or `echo "cd to [$DIR] failed."` as you like.

  — If using `set -u`, you will get an error if the variable is not defined—but not if it is defined but is just unexpectedly empty.

- Prefer single quotes around `printf` formats (see "POSIX Output" on page 56 and the rest of "Time for printf" on page 55).

Layout

- Line things up! Multiple spaces almost never matter in bash (except around =), and lining up similar commands makes it easier to read and to see both the similarities and differences.

- *Do not allow trailing white space!* This will later cause noise in the VCS (version control system) when removed.

- Indent using four spaces, but use TAB with here-documents as needed.

- Break long lines at around 78 columns, indent line continuations two spaces, and break just before | or > so those parts jump out as you scan down the code.

- The code to open a block goes on one line, like:

  — `if expression; then`

  — `for expression; do`

- List elements in `case..esac` are indented four spaces, and closing `;;` are at that same indent level. Blocks for each item are also indented four spaces.

  — One-line elements should be closed with `;;` on the same line.

  — Prefer lining up the `)` in each element, unless it gets cluttered or out of hand.

  — See the example code in Example 8-4.

Syntax

- Use `#!/bin/bash` - or `#!/usr/bin/env bash` when writing bash code, not `#!/bin/sh`.

- Use `$@` unless you are *really* sure you need `$*`.

- Use == instead of = for equality, to reduce confusion with assignment.

- Use $() instead of `` backticks/backquotes.

- Use [[instead of [(unless you need [for portability, e.g., dash).

- Use (( )) and $(( )) as needed for integer arithmetic; avoid let and expr.

- Use [[expression]] && block or [[expression]] || block when it is simple and readable to do so. Do not use [[expression]] && block || block because that doesn't do what you think it does; use if .. then .. (elif ..) else .. fi for that.

- Consider using "Unofficial bash Strict Mode" (see "Unofficial bash Strict Mode" on page 96).
  - set -euo pipefail will prevent or unmask many simple errors.
  - Watch out for this one, and use it carefully (if you use it at all): IFS=$'\n\t'.

Other

- For "system" scripts, log to syslog and let the OS worry about final destination(s), log rotation, etc.

- Error messages should go to STDERR, like echo 'A Bad Thing happened' 1>&2.

- Sanity-check that external tools are available using [-x /path/to/tool] || { ...error code block... }.

- Provide useful messages when things fail.

- Set exit codes, especially when you fail.

Script Template

```
#!/bin/bash -
# Or possibly: #!/usr/bin/env bash
# <Name>: <description>
# Original Author & date:
# Current maintainer?
# Copyright/License?
# Where this code belongs?  (Hosts, paths, etc.)
# Project/repo?
# Caveats/gotchas?
# Usage?  (Better to have `-h` and/or `--help` options!)
# $URL$  # If using SVN
ID=''    # If using SVN
#_____
PROGRAM=${0##*/}  # bash version of `basename`

# Unofficial bash Strict Mode?
```

```
#set -euo pipefail
### CAREFUL: IFS=$'\n\t'

# GLOBAL and constant variables are in UPPER case
LOG_DIR='/path/to/log/dir'

### Consider adding argument handling to YOUR template; see:
# examples/ch08/parseit.sh
# examples/ch08/parselong.sh
# examples/ch08/parselonghelp.sh


# Functions are in Mixed Case
##############################################################################
# Define functions


#----------------------------------------------------------------------------
# Example function
# Globals: none
# Input:    nothing
# Output:   nothing
function Foo {
    local var1="$1"
    ...
} # End of function foo



#----------------------------------------------------------------------------
# Another example function
# Globals: none
# Input:    nothing
# Output:   nothing
function Bar {
    local var1="$1"
    ...
} # End of function bar


##############################################################################
# Main

# Code...
```

Index

About the Authors

Carl Albing is a professor, researcher, and software engineer with a breadth of industry experience. A coauthor of O'Reilly's *bash Cookbook* and *Cybersecurity Ops with bash*, as well as the author of O'Reilly's "Great bash" video, Carl has worked in software (using bash and many other languages) for companies large and small, across a variety of industries. He has a BA in mathematics, a master's in international management (MIM), and a PhD in computer science.

JP Vossen has been working with computers since the early 80s and has been in the IT industry since the early 90s, specializing in information security since the late 90s. He's been fascinated with scripting and automation since he first understood what an autoexec.bat was, and was delighted to discover the power and flexibility of bash and GNU on Linux in the mid-90s. He has previously written for *Information Security Magazine* and *SearchSecurity*, among other publications. On those few occasions when he's not in front of a computer, he is usually taking something apart, putting something together, or both.

Colophon

The animal on the cover of *bash Idioms* is a harp shell (*Harpa articularis*). Commonly known as the articulate harp shell, it is a species of sea snail in the family Harpidae. The Harpidae family consists of about 55 species, the majority of which are found in the Indo-Pacific region, with only two of the species found in the coastal waters along the Baja Peninsula. This particular species, *Harpa articularis*, is found in shallow waters in the Indian Ocean and South Pacific, including as far as Fiji and the Australian coast. This species is known for the intricate scalloped patterns and colors of its shells, which range between 50 to 110 mm in size.

The Harpidae family can be identified by their smooth polished exterior. There are strong ribs running along the length of the shell, and the aperture is large and flared with a notch at the bottom. They do not have an operculum (a sheet-like structure that acts as a trapdoor for the snail inside, preventing the animal from drying up). Instead, the animal's large foot extends well beyond the edge of the shell.

Harp shells are nocturnal predators. They bury themselves in sand during the day and emerge at night to feed on crabs and shrimp. They feed by covering their prey with their foot and enveloping it in mucus. In turn, they can fall prey to larger crabs, fish, and predatory mollusks. In order to defend themselves, the harp shell uses a very interesting defense technique: it has the ability to amputate a rear portion of its foot, which continues to wiggle and distract the predator while the harp shell itself crawls away.

Many of the animals on O'Reilly covers are endangered; all of them are important to the world.

The cover illustration is by Karen Montgomery, based on an antique engraving from *Pictorial Museum of Animated Nature*. The cover fonts are Gilroy Semibold and Guardian Sans. The text font is Adobe Minion Pro; the heading font is Adobe Myriad Condensed; and the code font is Dalton Maag's Ubuntu Mono.

O'REILLY®

Learn from experts.
Become one yourself.

Books | Live online courses
Instant Answers | Virtual events
Videos | Interactive learning

Get started at oreilly.com.

Printed in the USA
CPSIA information can be obtained
at www.ICGtesting.com
JSHW050953140524
63053JS00009B/250

9 781492 094753